I0832046

EARL
Dr. W. B. Kellogg

AUTOBIOGRAPHY

OF

DR. D. B. KELLOGG

OR,

EXPLANATION OF CLAIRVOYANCE.

BEING AN ACCOUNT OF THE MYSTERIES OF HIS LIFE; COMBINED WITH A CONCISE EXPLANATION OF THE PHENOMENA OF CLAIRVOYANCE, SOMNAMBULISM, AND SPIRIT MANIFESTATION.

ANN ARBOR,
DR. CHASE'S STEAM PRINTING HOUSE.
1869.

PREFACE.

THIS AUTOBIOGRAPHY has been written in order to satisfy the urgent desire of my numerous friends, who believing, that there was something mysterious about me, have made frequent enquiry concerning the peculiarities of my life. For the last twelve years I have daily been asked the following questions, concerning the mystery of my professional practice, as a physician: "What is the cause of your influence?" "Are you a clairvoyant, or only a spirit medium?" "Did you study medicine before you commenced practice as a physician?" "Are clairvoyants always correct in their diagnosis of diseases?" "What are the principles of clairvoyance, and what is the formula of procedure necessary to development in this somnambulic science?" "Is not magnetism the basis of clairvoyance, of somnambulism, and of modern spirit communion?" "Were you, in early life, different from other children?" etc., etc. These questions I have endeavored to answer in a plain, concise manner.

I claim no literary merit for this production, for I make no professions of proficiency in the art of writing for publication.

Some of my explanations of the phenomena of magnetic operations differ from the conclusions of other writers upon the subject. But I feel that the careful investigators will not fail to see the philosophy of my views, particularly upon the subject of spirit communication. I have carefully avoided speaking of spiritualism as a religion, and have treated it only as a science. Of my early life I have said but little, and nothing of my domestic experience ; for I have considered that part of my life uninteresting to the general reader.

Some of my immediate friends have unqualifiedly asserted that this work was being written by a hired biographer. This supposition is emphatically erroneous. The whole work has been written by myself at odd spells during the last summer, and has been copied verbatim, by another party. Throughout the work I have aimed to treat exclusively of my magnetic career, and in my explanations I have endeavored to do nothing more than to show the philosophy of the phenomena treated.

Owing to the calculated compass of the work I have been forced to condense the matter into a compact form, hence, careful reading is necessary to a full understanding of the various subjects treated. I have not endeavored to build up any new faith, nor tare down any long standing theories, but have aimed, throughout the whole work, to answer such questions as have been most frequently asked me.

Trusting that would-be critics will show leniency toward me as a writer, I humbly hope that this work will meet the approbation of my patients and friends, and if it does, the only object sought will have been attained.

DR. DANIEL B. KELLOGG.

Ann Arbor, Mich., Dec. 20, 1868.

AUTOBIOGRAPHY.

CHAPTER I.

BIRTH, PARENTAGE, AND EARLY RECOLLECTIONS.

Warm from their spirit spreads around,
  An atmosphere serene—divine,—
Magnetical like golden haze,
  Encircling mine.

THE FIRST scene in the life drama about to be delineated, was enacted on the 22d of January, 1834, in a rough, uncouth, log-shanty, situated in the then sparsely settled town of Pittsfield, Washtenaw county, Michigan.

There was nothing worthy of remark or consideration in the exterior or interior of this particular edifice, unless it was its complete simplicity of structure. Being built of rough unhewn logs—with single slope to the roof—shanty style—from which protuded a massive stick-chimney. Its outside appearance was certainly in direct opposition to any cultivated ideal of magnificence; nor did its interior arrangements belie the uncouth appearances of its exterior in the least, for there was but one apartment, and this answered the combined purposes of parlor, kitchen, and sleeping apartment, in one. This rough and grotesque specimen of pioneer architecture has long since passed into oblivion, and even its surroundings have been robbed of their primitive wildness by the onward march of progressive husbandry.

I have no doubt but what I was considered a welcome addition to the family circle, and an object of parental gratification and love, though I do not imagine that my worthy parents saw anything about me above the plain of medriocrity of ability, yet I was a new link in the golden chain that united their hearts in conjugal felicity.

My conclusion that I was a welcome and cherished addition to the family fold is not altogether the result of instinctive supposition, which is innate in the heart of every child, but is a conclusion deduced from my matured observations and knowledge of the perfect conjugal felicity and noble characteristics of my respected parents, who considered the welfare of their offspring as the first great duty of life. Love for their children was, with them, an intrinsic virtue, ever flowing with unceasing power and beauty from then Christian hearts. Through all the various vicissitudes of life their love for their children, has glowed with the same warmth and golden luster as it did when they sang the soft lullaby to infant ears attuned.

I doubt whether there could be a more perfect matrimonial alliance than that enjoyed by my father and mother, nor one more conducive to wedded happiness. Still, strange and unphilosophical as the fact may appear to be, truth compells me to assert, that, in temperament and disposition, they were as unlike as is possible for two beings, bearing the image of their Creator, to be. My father was more than ordinarily positive in disposition and temperament, and he commanded respect by his indomitable force of will. In his domestic relations he was, in every sense, the acknowledged head, and his decisions on all questions of order, was admitted as authority from which there was no appeal. These positive characteristics of my worthy paternal progenitor were, in my childhood days, subjects of considerable speculation. I saw much about him that was entirely beyond my comprehension. In fact I looked upon my father as a sort of domestic tyrant; for it was patent to my childish mind that he was a bitter opposer to innocent amusement, and I considered this an inherent principle of his nature. But as I look back and contemplate his acts of apparent tyranny and domestic severity, I see that these characteristic traits were more assumed than natural, for they were the legitimate results of his peculiar moral and religious training which engendered a truly laudable desire to protect those under his control from the besetting sins of a sin-cursed world. He was, in the broad definition of the term, a Christian, and a thorough disciplinarian; not merely a professor of religion, but an unflinching, practical devotee of the church; who carried his religious ideas into every act of life. Nor were his religious principles the result of excited impulse, but were the convictions of deep study, of earnest thought, and laborious investigation; for, though in early life, he had enjoyed but poor educational advantages, his naturally vigorous mind had caused him to study many of the deep mysteries of human existence; and among his researches the various theological modes of future salvation claimed his attention most, for they were apparently most congenial to his peculiar turn of mind. But I am unable to state at what particular period of life his theological researches culminated in this professed avowal of Christian membership; still, I have reason to believe that his boyhood had ripened into manhood prior to the event, marked by his conversion to .Christianity.

Be this as it may. During the early years of my life my father was known in matters of religion as a zealous, unflinching, and uncompromising devotee of the church, who allowed his pious enthusiasm to carry him into the whirlpool of religious fanaticism to an extent sufficient to cause him to expend annually too much of his material profit, and even of his accumulated possessions in the cause of religious promulgation. In these days his landed possessions were quite extensive; and though his domains were wild and uncultivated, and in their primitive condition nonproductive and unprofitable for the time being, they were a sure foundation for future wealth. But year by year these broad acres were disposed of until at last they had, as if by magic; dwindled away to a single lot of 80 acres; and much, in fact nearly all the proceeds had been engulphed in the rapacious maw of the church, through the effect of thoughtless fanaticism.

Do not for a moment imagine that I would censure my father for his zealousness in religion, for though I condemn the act, the motive I am obliged to respect. His liberal endowment to the church was the result of studied conviction. He considered himself as a laborer in the vineyard of the Lord, and that the earth and fullness thereof was God's. He believed that the highest and first duty of a Christian was to freely expend the bounties given by the benificent Creator in promulgating his law by a free distribution of his sacred word, far and wide, among the benighted nations of the earth.

Yet, notwithstanding, the over zealousness in matters of religion, my father held the respect of all classes of people, even those who condemned his zeal or marked him as a fanatic, looked upon him as a man of good morals and practical business principles, with unswerving integrity and perfect purity of intention. Honesty in all business relations was the unvarying maxim of his life. Charity was the bright guiding star of his faith, and morality was the dictator of every act.

Although my father was sanguine even to fanaticism in his conviction of right and wrong, firmly adhering for a time to his opinions, and presistent in their advocacy; he was still liberally progressive. All theories were subjected by him to close analysis and uncompromising research, and whatever theory failed to pass through this ordeal of strict investigation, was cast aside without regret, regardless of the opinions of the uninvestigating masses, who often unjustifiably remarked him as being unstable. Even theology was subjected to this guiding principle of his life, as all who are acquainted with his Christian career can testify. "Isms" were adopted and advocated with all the strenuous powers of his mind, only to be cast aside in exchange for something more in accordance with the dictates of reason, until he finally, had made the circuit of nearly all the modern methods of salvation. But throughout the whole of his Christian career, varying and changable as appearances may indicate that career to have been, no one could honestly accuse him of being actuated by any mercenary motives, or anything outside of the pure dictates of conscience governed by reason.

That my father was unstable I cannot deny; but this instability was in consequence of an inate desire for truth. His mind was continually reaching out after something which would harmonize with the interior purity of his own mind, and accord with what reason said was right. He was mentally positive and self-reliant, and this outstretching after greater truths was an inherent and irresistable principle of his life.

I have said that my parents were opposite, or unlike in temperament and disposition. That my father commanded respect and obedience by his perfect moral life and indomnitable power of will. On the other hand, my mother won the love of her associates by her natural kindness and affability of manner. Her acts were the spontaneous product of a heart naturally pure; and were always deeds of thoughtful kindness. So clinging, vine-like, were her affections, so passive her mental powers, and confiding her love, that she was by nature constrained to grant willing acquiescence to the more positive dictates of my father's will, and by this course she won not only his respect but the warmest affections of his stern and positive nature. Nor was this all, for this native meekness won for her the kindness of all who came in the radius of her pure influence. To her children she was indulgent to the near proximity of a fault. Her love for them was boundless, and her endeavors to make their lives radiant with the sunshine of a happy home, was considered as the highest duty of her life, and for her deeds of unselfish maternal kindness she had the proud satisfaction of receiving the purest love and warmest affection of her entire family as well as their willing obedience to her passive maternal authority. While my father governed his household by stern and unswerving principles, which were the result of his ideas of morality and religion, my mother ruled alone by principles dictated by love emanating from a heart of purity.

I doubt whether there could have been a better

combination of powers for controlling wayward youth. I respected my father for his methodical principles of justice and close adherance to moral training, but I loved my mother for her pure unselfish affection which was ever displaying itself by some thoughtful deed of maternal kindness. One, won obedience and respect by the power of moral example, the other, by the supreme power of reciprocal affection.

I refer to these facts in regard to the unlikeness of disposition and temperament characteristic of my parents, in order that the reader may understand my hereditary proclivities. While my father was mentally and physically positive, my mother in both of these respects was decidedly negative; and as like begets like, I partook largely of the two casts of temperaments natural to my parents. Mentally I am like my father, physically like my mother; and this fact readily accounts for much of the mystery of my life; for it furnishes a clue to the psychological phenomena connected with my career.

The early years of my life were characteristicly like those which fall to the lot of all boys who are reared amid the scenes of pioneer life; and may be said to have been made up of sunshine and gloom. When I was free from that pest of frontier life, the fever and ague, I was a being of perfect contentment, and my days were days of unalloyed happiness. But during the first five years of my existence, t' ese days of freedom from the above mentioned malady, were extremely few in number; in fact, I was almost continually under the alternate frigid and torrid influences of this fell destroyer of backwoods happiness. Malarious disease appeared to be indisolubly connected with my existence, and in view of this fact my parents almost despaired of hoping to see me arrive to the statue of manhood. But at the age of five there came a change in my physical health, and from that time I began to develop into a healthy robust youth; from this time forth I was allowed the freedom of out-door exercise, and this unwonted privilege I enjoyed with boyish gusto.

During these early years, my only playmate, and almost constant companion was my sister Harriet, who was two years my senior, and who, in consideration of this variance in age, practically considered herself to be my natural guide and guardian. With her I roamed the dense forests which surrounded our home, with the freedom of a native denizen of the woods; and although our amusements could not boast of the polish of city elegance, and hardly of civilization, still they were both instructive and healthy; and though I knew nothing of marbles and such frivolous means of enjoyment, I was, even in my sixth year, an expert with the bow and arrow, and many were the specimens of feathered beauty that I brought my loved sister—who was ever proud of my hunting achievements—as trophies of my skill. Thus, in the enjoyment of wild and unconventional childhood, time flitted unconsciously by, utterly devoid of unusual events, until the seventh year of my life.

During the summer following my seventh birthday, various domestic arrangements, differing from the usual routine, were planned and executed. Early in the summer my father—who was never blessed with a very well developed faculty of continuity or locality—was attacked with one of his periodical and irresistible longings for a change of residence. All former experience had proven that there was no known panacea for this species of mental derangement; and the consequent result of the attack was a speedy exchange of home. But, unlike most former removes, this one proved to be quite satisfactory to all concerned; for not only was the distance short, but we exchanged the old dilapidated shanty for an edifice of comparative elegance; for though built of logs, its exterior was more prepossessing, and its interior more commodious and comfortable. My time would have passed as pleasantly in this new home as it had in the old, had not that bug-bear of early childhood—school-house imprisonment—reared its freedom-destroying prospects to view. Bitterly I detested the idea of exchanging my boyish freedom—my romping, wild-wood sports, for the monotony of district school. I had learned enough of my sister's experience—who had attended one term—to establish in my mind a conviction of hatred for study, and the irksome inactivity of early school life. So deep-seated was this conviction, and so permanent was my antipathy, that I earnestly begged my parents not to send me. In my own heart, I remember that I then considered ignorance far preferable to the horrid task of acquiring education by the means in prospect; and I frankly told my parents that I did not want to learn, I begged they would not send me to school, but let me grow up in ignorance. Of what use was education to me. Books could not learn me how to direct my arrows so as to bring down the winged inhabitant of the air, and beyond these rustic sports my mind had never extended. But of course my entreaties were useless, and my preferred alternative was made by my father the basis of a long lecture, perfectly incomprehensible at the time, on the benefits of education. The upshot of the whole was that, on commencement day, I found myself occupying one of the hard wooded benches in the old log schoolhouse, as a primary student.

My school days were the real commencement of my life; for during them I took my first draught from the bitter cup of experience. To be sure, these early troubles were comparatively insignificant, and so are all the sorrows of early childhood. No child ever abhorred study more than I. It was almost impossible for me to commit a lesson to memory, and in consequence, I was considered by the old hawk-eyed pedagogue as a regular dolt; and as a thick-headed numbskull by all the precocious youngsters of my own age. My place in the class was a permanent position—being the foot—which, by long continued occupancy, I came to consider mine, without the least feeling of compunction or twinge of shame. But, notwithstanding I was a thick-headed, dull, unadvancing student at school, and a despiser of education, there were some traits of my mental character that were decidedly prominent and well developed, and among these was a well cultivated propensity for mischief. This trait was not only a source of annoyance to my teacher and school-fellows, but to all who had anything to do with me, and especially those who happened to incur my displeasure. Many were the pranks I played upon my school-fellows in payment for their too liberal use of obnoxious appellations. I knew that in matters of education I was below ordinary, but it cut me to the quick to be told that I was an ignoramus, especially by those whom I knew were no way my superiors in anything outside of books. This propensity for mischief often annoyed my kind-hearted mother, and shocked the strict methodical principles of my father. Nothing was exempt from this natural fondness for fun; even the old house-dog and the quiet, inoffensive cat came in for their share of torment, much in opposition to their trained habits of puritanical decorum. On one occasion, I remember, this mischeivous propensity placed me in rather an awkward predicament, which, as it is a fair specimen of my boyish capers, I will relate.

On this occasion the family had just seated themselves for breakfast, and my father was engaged in making his usual appeal for divine blessing upon the food prepared for the nourishment of the body, and just as he was giving utterance to the clause wherein he prayed "that the strength gained therefrom might be spent in glorifying the Almighty," I, who had been watching affairs from without, rushed into the room with a large cow-bell suspended from my neck, on entering I combined with the horrid rattle-clatter of the bell, a ludicrous imitation of bovine bellowing. The effect was as instantaneous as an electric shock, and was manifested by a suppressed giggle from the elder part, and an explosive outburst of mirth from the younger portion of the family. Of course, I was perfectly conscious of the outrageousness of my conduct, and fully expected a peremptory dismissal from the room, in connection with a fierce promise of speedy punishment in return for my wanton disrespect of the sanctity of the occasion. But for once in my life, I was happily deceived; for contrary to all precedent, and my own expectation, my father caught the infection of mirth. Cutting short his appeal for divine blessing, he gave vent to his irrepressible convictions of the ludicrous, and for a few moments indulged in an unwonted fit of laughter. But notwithstanding this, to me, happy termination of the affair, my father did not fail to warn me of an altogether different style of consequences in case of a repetition of my conduct. This warning was long remembered and referred to whenever my mischeivous inclinations prompted me to indulge in any pranks at his expense. Thus my early life was passed, and consisted mostly of well-earned punishment for childish indiscretion. Mischief was my greatest study, and in this branch I became a proficient. Still, I do not imagine that my early years were greatly unlike the life of other boys who chance, like me, to be the victims of puritanical sanctimoniousness. The greatest fault laid with my father, who believed that even childish amusements were obnoxious to the Almighty, and an offense against religion.

CHAPTER II.

BEING AN ACCOUNT OF NERVOUS PECULIARITIES, AND INCIPIENT MANIFESTATIONS OF CLAIRVOYANCE.

AS A series of common-place events characterize my individual career between the eighth and fifteenth years of my life, I will pass them unnoticed. But during this period, there had been much change in the general aspect of my surroundings. Progressive improvement in branches of industry was apparent on all sides; and now, instead of wild and uncultivated "woodland copse," were seen on every hand

> "Deep waving fields, and pastures green,
> With gentle slopes and vales between."

Comparative affluence had taken the place of pioneer penury, and as display is the inevitable associate of prosperity, society had brushed and polished itself into a sort of rustic elegance. Villages, which could boast commercial importance, had sprung into existence as if by magic.

Childhood had grown to youth, and youth had donned the regal rights of manhood. Even my father's domestic arrangements had undergone a progressive change. The old log house, in which I had passed many happy days, had gone into oblivion, and on its former site now stood a more elegant structure of brick. And the old log school-house, with its rough, hard benches, had likewise fallen victim to the prevalent spirit of improvement; and its place was now adorned with a more imposing edifice; and even the old hawk-eyed domine, of bitter recollections, was laid up as superanuated, and was looked upon as one of the fossil remains of another age; and in pursuance with the growing pride of the neighborhood, his place was now occupied by a spruce specimen of young America, in broadcloth. In short, general improvement was everywhere manifest.

At the age of fifteen I looked upon myself, in physical sense, as a pretty good specimen of a man; but I was painfully aware that my mental advancement had not kept corresponding pace with my physical growth. I knew that I had a natural incapacity for learning; and though I studied hard, I had, up to this time, made no progress beyond the primary branches of English education. Evidently, book-learning was not my forte; and as this fact had become patent to my Father, he gave up all ideas,—if he ever indulged any—of giving me more than ordinary advantages of education. My summers were, during these years, spent in labor on the farm; and though I attended school two winter terms after I was fifteen, I accomplished but little more in that time than a review of my former studies. Thus, at the conclusion of my school days, I was considered below par in the legally defined branches of even primary education; and from that time to the present, I have never entered any institution of learning as a student. But, notwithstanding the fact that I made this slow progress in acquiring the fundamental principles of defined education, my mind was continually undergoing a process of vigorous development, by an intuitive acquirement of intelligence, from nature's inexhaustible fountain of knowledge. There was something about me, at this time, which was remarkably peculiar. I was unlike the general class; for though I could not learn from books, I experienced no trouble in arriving at a knowledge of the attributes of whatever came before my observation. My mind appeared to be susceptible to intuitive knowledge. I was habitually a close observer and investigator of all objective formation, and in my own mind, I was conscious of possessing strange analytic powers. But while I recognized this peculiar individual capacity, or gift, I was wholly unable to account for it; and in view of this fact, I durst not divulge the secret, and for me to give an explanation of the phenomena was literally impossible at that time; for I could not tell how, or by what means, or from whence the power was derived. Besides, I then supposed that I was not unlike the rest of mankind. I knew nothing of the principles of clairvoyance—even the term was foreign to my vocabulary. I was conscious that I possessed a strange power, on some occasions, of mental penetration, combined with a sort of natural exaltation of understanding and analytic ability. But why I was so I could not tell. It was only on rare occasions that I outwardly manifested these strange gifts, for I had no desire to attract the attention of the curious. One special result of this insipient clairvoyant development of my mental and physical organism, and one which I outwardly manifested most, was an ability to predict impending atmospheric changes. This I would often do with unerring accuracy, and to the astonishment of even my most confidential friends; and not only would I prognosticate a change of weather, but would, with perfect correctness, specify the time and peculiar kind of change about to occur, long before there would be any visible signs, apparent to the common observer, of an atmospheric variation. People wondered not a little at this display of apparent prophetic powers, and there were many superstitious persons who imaginged that I was endowed with supernatural powers of discernment. I was a mystery even to myself; for I did not understand the principle of this peculiar power, nor why I should differ so materially from the rest of mankind, until long after, when the mystery was explained by the discovery that I was unconsciously a clairvoyant.

These prophecies—if such they may be termed—were the result of clairvoyant powers in their undeveloped stage, or primary conditions, hence were closely allied to nervous sensation. My nervous organization, being naturally negative, was sensibly affected by even the slightest change of atmosphere, and thus I was naturally a sort of human barometer.

But being a human weathercock did not, even in these early days, fully comprehend the extent of my unusual abilities, for I could, with perfect ease, place myself in magnetic connection with other elements of the universe; could, when in proper condition, determine the properties of liquid, and even of solid bodies, by simply holding them in the hollow of my hand. At these times my mind seemed to be exalted, and my power of perception and penetration were capable of increase beyond their normal state. I often wondered at this phenomena, and as I said nothing of the mystery of my nature, I had considerable curiosity to know if I was really unlike the great mass of mankind, or were they, like myself, holding a portion of their natural powers a secret from the world.

The reader will bear in mind that my clairvoyant powers were undeveloped at this date. I was not endowed at this time with perfect vision, nor could I wander off in mental freedom, and place myself in rapport with distant objects, as I do at this date of my clairvoyant experience. My physical nerves were then the only channel through which intelligence could be borne to my mind. I was not unlike others; only in extreme nervous sensitiveness did I vary from the rest of mankind. My powers of predicting atmospheric changes, and of determining the elementary properties of different bodies, was the legitimate result of peculiar nervous construction. The extreme sensitiveness of my nervous system was perceptibly agitated by every variation of atmospheric elements;

and these perceptible changes of nervous feeling were subjects of mental analysis, and in every instance conclusions were the result of calculations induced by nervous effect. Thus, a feeling of mental langour and cerebral exhaustion foreshadowed a storm; a prickly, nervous sensation was a certain indication of wind; and so I experienced a physical sign for every atmospheric variation, more or less intense, according to the mildness or severity of the change about to occur. Bodies held in the hand would cause a perceptible electric sensation, which varied in accordance with the elementary constituents of the article grasped. Bodies that were powerfully impregnated with iron would ofttimes emit a powerful electric shock, and at other times I could handle the same article without experiencing even the slightest nervous sensation. At times, liquids poured in the palm of my hand would powerfully agitate my whole nervous system, and these phenomena were in consequence of magnetic sympathy. I was, even in these boyhood days, a powerful magnet to vital electricity; and though this was before I had any practical knowledge of the phenomena of spirit communication by means of electric "raps," I was often startled by unaccountable electric sounds in strange proximity to my person. Evidently, these "sounds" were caused by the confined electricity of my system seeking its equilibrium in the external atmosphere; but in these days I could give no reason for the mystery, consequently the phenomena was an annoying, though incomprehensible subject of individual speculation. And thus, even in my early life, I was a mystery even to myself, and an object of wonder among my friends.

CHAPTER III.

MY FIRST SORROW, AND MY FIRST ACQUAINTANCE WITH MAGNETISM.

Many years have passed and weary,
Since they laid her down to rest,
In the grave-yard, lone and dreary,
With the cold clods on her breast.

IN THE summer of my seventeenth year occurred the first sorrowful episode of my life. My sister, Harriet, whom I have said was my constant companion during early life, and who in later years had been my most cherished counselor, and adviser, and confidant—she of all my kindred I loved the most, was suddenly stricken down by the destroying power of a fatal miasmatic disease. Never shall I forget the feeling of perfect loneliness which thrilled through my heart when I came to realize the extent and finality of my bereavement. This was my first personal knowledge of death. Oh! how bitter were the tears I shed, when in the solemn hush of night I stood with the family group beside the sufferer's couch, to behold the immortal spirit break the frail cord that bound it to its still beautiful form of dying clay. There was just one throe of mortal pain—one lingering, conscious glance of perfect love for mourning friends around, which sent an electric thrill of anguish through each sorrowing heart—one flutter of the dying heart, and she was dead! And after this there followed the solemn panoply of death, and one bright and beautiful morning—a morning musical with the joyous songs of birds—they bore the coffined form away through the sunlight, and hid it among the moss grown groves and white memorials of departed life. And now, though

Many years have passed and weary,
Since they laid her down to rest,
In the grave-yard, lone and dreary,
With the cold clods on her breast.
Many times the flowers have faded,
By the column at her head,
Since the grave her brow hath shaded
And they called our loved one dead.
But I cannot find her sleeping
In that shadow-haunted spot,
Where the myrtle wreath is creeping
Round the sweet forget-me-not.

No, ah no! beneath the willow,
They have laid the casket down;
But the grave is not her pillow,
Nor her bed the damp, cold ground.
For beyond the silent river
And the swaying willow bough,
Free from sorrow—now and ever—
With a crown upon her brow,
I behold her, angel risen;—
She has left the lowly spot
That her body still doth prison,
'Neath the sweet forget-me-not.

As I have said, this bereavement was my first cause of real, lasting sorrow; and for a long time my grief bowed me to the dust, for I could not but remember that in my idolized sister's death I had lost a true friend that could never be replaced.

This mournful episode of early death was likewise —young as I was—the cause of much religious thought; for somehow, I could not rid myself of the idea that there existed a great inharmony between the native promptings of the human heart and the sophistry of church-taught religion. I had been taught, by my father, that only those who were born again, and sanctified through the gracious mercy of an offended God, could hope to inherit eternal happiness. I had been led to believe that if there was no outward show of spirit sanctification by active, ceaseless praying, that eternal condemnation would be an inevitable consequence. My loved sister, I knew had never manifested any faith in, or regard for these religious qualifications. She had lived, an unsophisticated child of nature, with a mind unclouded by care, or even a thought of the mysterious future upon which she had thus prematurely entered. But still I could not believe that she, who had never been guilty of an intentional wrong act—whose heart alone pulsated with purest love for all of God's creatures, was now by the Almighty condemned to eternal damnation, merely because she had made no profession of sanctity, or proclaimed, by formal prayer, heart-felt praise to the Almighty.

Nay, in my own heart, I could but believe her an angel now, in the realms of the eternal summer-land.

As these convictions took hold of my mind, there arose a feeling of disrespect for that heartless and cold religion which taught, thus-wise, that the unerring child of God was by nature doomed to eternal punishment for the transgression of others. From this time, the prayers of my pious father appeared like mockery, and fell coldly upon my heart.

These individual convictions were not the only consequences of this heart-felt bereavement; for I have reason to believe that from this time forth, my father began to discern that there was a great inharmony between the so-called will of God and the natural promptings of the God-created heart of man; for from this time his faith was apparently shaken in his former creeds. For a time his mind wandered darkly among the bewildering isms of theology, now grasping—as dying men will grasp at straws—the flimsy formula of some inspirational faith, only to cast it aside as unsatisfactory. Thus, for a time, was he in the gloom of spiritual darkness, surrounded by doubts and misgivings. Alas! why will mankind persist in declaring the human soul—the image of God in man—as under a curse eternal? How many poor, striving mortals have lived and died, believing that a life of purity would avail them nought in the land of spirits! How many have died, believing that the pearly gates were closed against them because they were not members of Christ's Church on earth. How often are we told by the learned man of God that our heart is but a charnel house of sin, and by nature prone only to evil. Can we wonder at the prevalence of evil and immorality among men who are taught that they are by nature vile—outcast from the love of God? Can we expect sweet water from a bitter fountain, or good results from evil intentions? Can we wonder at infidelity, when fidelity rests alone upon the flimsy hypothesis of second birth, or change of heart, in a manner so mysterious as to be almost, if not entirely, beyond human understanding? We know the human mind is ever active—ever producing good or bad results; then how much more noble and God-like—for He pronounced all things good—it is to consider the heart as the fountain of goodness, rather than a natural cess-pool of iniquity. Good deeds are the ruling effects of every human being. Evil acts are alone the exception. Man is by nature good; by education evil. When will Christians break down this stupendous error, this blasphemous libel on the goodness of God, this mountain of falsehood, this bug-bear of natural sin; and teach instead, that man is the noblest handiwork of Omniscient power, whose heart is, in the image of his Creator, naturally pure; whose greatest aim should be to keep it as it came from the fountain, free from the contamination of evil?

During the winter following my sister's death, our quiet rural district was visited by a noted itinerant expositor of mesmerism, who announced that he would exhibit his wonderful experiments at the district school-house for several consecutive nights. Of course, the sober denizens of these extremely quiet precincts were attacked with an irresistible desire to view the strange phenomena, and those who had a glimmer of its real import, were anxious to be conveyed into the mysterious slumber. My father was terribly sceptical about the correctness and utility of the professor's boasted magnetic power. He did not, however, refuse me the privelege, nor deny himself the pleasure of attending. Accordingly, on the first evening of mesmeric display the professor was greeted by a full house of anxious expectants. Perhaps there was none present who had more curiosity than I; for even the term mesmerism was an undefined something wholly beyond my knowledge. After a miserable display of third-rate oratory, which did not have the remotest tendency to enlighten my mind upon the subject, the professor proceeded to a practical demonstration of the grand magnetic mystery.

Having placed a lighted candle in the most conspicuous position possible, he directed that those who desired magnetic effect should keep their gaze riveted thereon for a specified number of minutes. This requirement I followed as implicitly as my understanding would permit. The operator now commenced a series of motions resembling the pantomime of "Legerdemain performers." These motions had a peculiar effect on my muscular system. My eyes displayed a decided tendency to close ; I was also conscious of a prickly sensation—a feeling of numbness in different parts of my body. I soon allowed my eyes to close, for I found that to keep them open was next to impossible. I felt no alarm at the strangeness of my feelings, for I was still perfectly cognizant of what was transpiring around me, and had full control of my mental powers. Besides, I erroneously supposed that all present experienced like feelings. The operator now came up to me, and after making a few passes in front of my face, he imperiously said—"You can't open your eyes." "I guess you are mistaken, old fellow," thought I; but I found, after a desperate effort, that he had spoken truth. I now became suddenly alarmed; for the thought occurred to me that perhaps I had forever lost the power of sight. But my fears were very soon dissipated, for on his touching the lids and commanding me to open them, they were unsealed without any apparent personal effort.

The professor now proceeded to demonstrate his mesmeric powers by magnetically controlling different members of my body. First my legs were placed under control, and rendered unserviceable to my individual will. So complete was the operator's control of them that he would force them to move in spite of my most strenuous opposition. My limbs being relieved, the influence was transferred to my arms; which were, by the same mysterious power, held in an extended position, in spite of my will to the contrary. Next followed a perversion of the sense of taste. I was made to eat tabacco, under the supposition that it was delicious candy. In the same manner, water was transferred or changed to wine, and from wine to bitterest gall. In each case the deception was astonishingly perfect.

During these performances I was conscious of the real condition of things, but had no power to do otherwise than as commanded by the operator. Though I knew it was tobacco I was eating, instead of candy, my taste agreed with the deception, and had I been blind and bereft of the sense of feeling, I would have sworn it was real candy I ate.

On this occasion my nervous sensations were similar to those induced by an electric battery. I could distinctly feel the operator's chilly hand pass and repass the subjected members, as bearing along with them an electric current. The living blood in my veins seemed well nigh arrested. All the nervous avenues of sensation were thrilled with quick flashes of electric fire, and at times a strange feeling agitated my brain; and once I came near losing sensorial power. The coldness of death appeared to settle upon those parts which were under the magnetic power or influence.

During the professor's stay in the neighborhood I was several times used as a subject upon which to test the authenticity of the science of mesmerism. The favorite mode of testing was for the operator to powerfully influence my hands, when incredulous observers were allowed to lacerate the flesh with pins and other sharp instruments, which they could do without my feeling any sensation of pain.

During these exhibitions I was never influenced beyond a partial state of psychology. I here note the fact in order to correct a prevalent opinion, that I was at this time developed as a clairvoyant, which some individuals have unqualifiedly asserted to be the case. This first psychological event of my life made an ineffaceable impression upon my mind; for it unfolded a new subject for contemplation. I discovered that I was not the independent and self-sufficient creature I had pictured myself to be. I found that there existed a governing power, strange, wonderful and inscrutible, and though unseen it was mighty and potent. I had learned by experience that I was subject to this power, evidently to a greater extent than the most of mankind. Here was an individual who could rob my mental powers of their legitimate rights, and control my physical organism in spite of my opposing will. Hours of deep thought were spent in a vain endeavor to unravel the mystery; but all my enquiries resulted in harassing conjectures and improbable theories concerning the power of mind over matter.

CHAPTER IV.

MY FIRST INFLUENCE AS A MEDIUM.

ABOUT THIS time the mysterious manifestations known as the "Rochester rappings" were, in consequence of their purporting to emanate from disembodied spirits, attracting considerable attention. Contrary to the expectation of nearly every one, who naturally looked upon the raps as some clever trick of legerdemain, or incomprehensible seven-day novelty that would soon die a natural death,the phenomena had kept gradually developing into new phases, until at this time it had, from an insignificant *rap*, grown to be a medium of inspirational intelligence. Claiming natural instead of supernatural emanation, according to fixed principles of natural law. A certain class of philosophers had, since the first rap in 1848, endeavored to argue the phenomenon out of existence, on the ground that there was no similitude as precedent laid down by any of the famous expounders of "things that be." Others claimed that it was a new phase of animal magnetism; and still another class scoffed at, and unqualifiedly pronounced the whole thing humbuggery.

But despite the condemnation of book-wise philosophers, the scoffs of ignorant ranters, or even the denunciations of horrified divines, the mysterious phenomena had moved steadily on, gaining each day in popular favor and interest.

Owing to the strangeness and unprecedented mystery of these so-called spirit manifestations, and rapidly increasing popularity, they had become a subject of interest and frequent discussion by the investigating and liberal-minded members of the community where I resided. Among the investigators my father was conspicuous; for since his divergence from the beaten paths of his former theological creeds, he had cultivated a liberality of principle to such extent that now truth was acceptable from whatever source it might emanate; and although he gave but little credence to the floating rumors concerning these purported spirit manifestations, he publicly admitted himself susceptible to any convictions that might be derived from practical investigation. Residing in the neighborhood was one other individual, a Mr. Ball, who was equally with my father solicitous of practically testing the truth or falsity of these mysterious visitations of spirits from the other world. Hence, in order to put their desires in execution, they, with other liberal-minded individuals, arranged to meet at an appointed time at my father's residence, for the purpose of inaugurating a series of practical tests.

Accordingly, in pursuance of this preconcerted arrangement, some half-score of earnest individuals convened to witness what might be received in the way of spirit demonstration. On this occasion Mr. Ball acted as master of ceremonies, and was allowed to make such arrangements and disposition of means as conformed with his ideas of the *modus operandi* required to bring about the hoped for result. These arrangements were extremely simple. An ordinary dining-table was placed so as to be accessible from all sides; then of the company those who were supposed to be susceptible of magnetic influence were chosen for members of the circle, and were instructed to place their hands on the table in such a manner as to form an endless chain or connection.

In consideration of my known susceptibility to mesmeric control, I was, contrary to my wishes, urged to become one of the mediumistic circle. To tell the truth, I had not a particle of faith in these purported spirit demonstrations, and I honestly believed the whole thing to be an absurd trick or else "humbug." I did not believe that these proceedings would result in anything but failure; consequently I unwillingly acquiesced with their wish, and took my place among the rest of the chosen ones. My preconceived ideas of complete failure were, during the first trial, somewhat modified. For after the elapse of some half-hour of passive quietness, I became suddenly conscious of a feeling of numbness gradually creeping along the nervous avenues of my hands and arms; which rapidly increased in power and intensity, sufficiently to cause spasmodic contraction of the muscles and cause my hands to move about in a highly fantastic manner. These uncontrolled gyrations were kept up for some time; but finally, on a piece of chalk being placed in reach, their fantastic irregularity of motion was considerably modified. So much so, in fact, that I was enabled to unconsciously write a few words in an intelligible manner. But by far the larger portion of these "chalk" manifestations consisted of unintelligible scrawls and hieroglyphics. No other demonstration was received at this sitting; nor did any other member of the circle recognize even the slightest sensation or influence.

But, notwithstanding these manifestations came far short of expectation, in point of interest or self-sustaining evidence of origin or utility, it was resolved by those present to continue the investigation, in hopes of better results in future. For, to use their own language, "if I had not been humbuging them, there was a prospect of my becoming a medium," and of their investigating the phenomena through me. This covert expression of doubt, of genuineness of manifestation, did not trouble me in the least, for I was completely mystified, and had very serious doubt of my own, though different in nature. For, while I was positive I used no deception or personal volition, I doubted the source from whence the controlling power emanated. It was supposed by those present that if the manifestations were foreign to myself, that is, if they were not the result of personal volition, that they were the effect of some mysterious spirit power.

But where was the proof that such was the case? Might not the power to produce these magnetic manifestations (for they were in physical kind the same in sensation and effect as I had experienced when magnetized), have emanated from those with whom I was connected. Mr. Ball had of late, on several occasions, placed me under his magnetic control, possibly he might have been the unconscious mesmeric cause on this occasion. In view of the plausibility of this inferred probability, I resolved to practically test the subject by some means or other.

Some week or ten days later, an opportnnity offered for making the desired test. On this occasion, I was on an evening visit to an aunt's, when the subject of spiritualism was broached, and followed by a proposition to form a circle, which was unanimously agreed to. With the exception of my aunt, those present were all persons of nearly my own age; in view of which fact I felt confident that if we realized any influence there could be no danger or probability of any local emanation of cause. Not one of the entire company had any known inductive mesmeric power. I had in my own mind become almost fully persuaded that my former sensation had been the result of an involuntary mesmeric power, emanating in an unconscious current from Mr. Ball. I was therefore astonished when, after a few moments of quiet, to again become conscious of the same mysterious influence. On this occasion, instead of fantastic movements, and unintelligible chalk marks, words, and finally complete sentences were written with neatness and astonishing rapidity, and before the close of this seance I had become sufficiently developed so that I could unconsciously answer even mental queries with astonishing correctness. During the entire performance I watched with interest the involuntary manœuvres of my hand. I had no knowledge or premonition of what was going to be written. My hand would involuntarily answer queries by writing, while I was otherwise mentally engaged in conversation on topics entirely foreign to those of which I wrote.

My former belief that the influence emanated from local powers or living agencies, was on this occasion completely overcome by unimpeachable evidence. But I still doubted the hypothesis that the influence was the result of spirit power. I was in a state of mental mystification, for I had been taught that when man died he went to a bourne from which return was impossible. But how else could I define the phenomenon? Was I the victim of Satanic incantation, or mental hallucination? Was it witchcraft, or some unknown mystery of natural law? In vain I strove to reach a plausible conclusion—to establish in my mind a theory that would be sustainable by reason or logic; but my thoughts were invariably lost in profound mystery. At last I resolved to continue my investigation until the light of truth should remove the clouds of mystery from my mental vision.

A few evenings later I was again influenced, this time at my father's residence, in presence of those who had first witnessed my mediumistic abilities. On this occasion the nature of my mediumistic proceedings was entirely unlike the two preceding manifestations, and consisted of physical tests. First, the raps were introduced, with undeniable distinctness. These were followed by some marvelous demonstrations of spirit power. Chairs, and other articles of furniture were caused to move without any perceptible assistance; and once, while my hands alone rested on the table, it was suddenly tipped to an inclined position, and held against the opposing power of four strong men, who, with united strength, endeavored to replace it.

During all these proceedings, I was only conscious of a powerful magnetic sensation, which appeared to flow from me towards such objects as were employed as means for manifestation. I was conscious of receiving and imparting a strong magnetic current, which, when not imparted caused a nervous tremor, similar to those caused by an induction of a current of electricity; but while this magnetic current was passing off, the tremor would entirely cease. In view of these facts, I reasonably consideded myself only as a medium of some foreign power; but my mind was still in the dark, as thus far I had received no convincing proof of intelligence being connected with the cause of the phenomena, hence I was not yet prepared to admit the theory of spirit emanation.

CHAPTER V.

MY ENTREE INTO THE THIRD MAGNETIC DEGREE.

Can such things be,
And overcome us like a summer's shower,
Without our special wonder?

IN ORDER not to tire the patience of my readers by delineations of similar events, I will hasten to detail the impressions that I received while in my first condition of clairvoyance. Prior to this occasion, I had twice been thrown into a somnambulic state—a condition of ultra-unconsciousness—through which I surmise all clairvoyants must pass ere they reach the third magnetic degree. These two events are blanks in my remembrance—moments of complete mental darkness—an undefinable cavity in my mental existence.

On the occasion in question, I passed through this veil of magnetic darkness into the bright realms of the third magnetic degree. I had but slight knowledge of the mysteries of magnetism; of the phenomena of clairvoyance I was almost entirely ignorant, having no clear conception of any such condition. But I was, on this occasion, borne by an unseen power into this mystic magnetic state in less than twenty minutes. After a few moments of mental and physical inertia, which was rather pleasant than otherwise, my mind passed into a delightful state of mental tranquility. My thoughts were extremely peaceful. I viewed with unutterable emotions of gladness a mental vision of happiness. I contemplated the principles of friendship and of universal love. My soul seemed to expand with mighty powers of penetration. I was not conscious that these mental prospects awakened the least heart-felt emotion; they appeared as ideas coming from an unknown fountain of intelligence. During these moments I was conscious of being enveloped in impenetrable darkness. Therefore, my conclusions were that I was in a deep physical sleep, mentally engaged in a peaceful revery. Soon I discovered that this conclusion was incorrect; for as my powers were expanded and enlarged, I saw that surrounding objects were glowing with illuminating tints, more or less brilliant and magnetical.

The figure of each person was enveloped in a light atmosphere, which emanated from it. I farther discovered that every tangible object emitted a luminous glow, which varied in degrees of brightness and magnitude. Animate objects were enveloped in more extensive and brilliant atmosphere than were inanimate. The former seemed to send forth ever varying tints, while the latter appeared as changeless in aspect. The utter novelty of this view overwhelmed my mind with astonishment and admiration. In vain I tried to comprehend this unprecedented phenomenon. I was completely confounded; and for a while I imagined that the earth and its inhabitants had been suddenly translated into a brilliant paradise. I could employ no language to describe my perceptions; hence, I viewed the magnificent scene with feelings of unutterable joy and reverence. But I had not yet reached the ultimate of my perceptive power. A few moments later I discovered that, by means of my new powers of mental penetration, I could observe with perfect ease the internal organization of every person in the room; could easily discern from whence emanated these magnetical exhalations that were so luminous.

All the organs of the human viscera—the liver, the spleen, the heart, the brain—were accessible to my mental inspection. The whole body appeared as a transparent sheet of glass, invested with strange, rich spiritual beauty. Every separate organ was the center of a brilliant illumination, peculiar to itself. Permeating the body throughout, in fact, it appeared as the body itself, was an unvarying flash of light; I soon recognized this as being the nervous fluid; and that *all* the other organs depended on this for means of activity. I saw that the air-chambers of the lungs were like chemical laboratories, causing instantaneous chemical changes in the blood which flowed through the contiguous membranes. The spinal column appeared as an unceasing stream of electric fire, and the brain as a reservoir of brilliant electric tints. Here, the phenomena was more varied than in any other portion of the organism. In fact, the emanation from each separate brain in the room displayed individuality. In other respects they were all nearly alike; but in this there was a marked difference. I afterward discovered the difference to be the effect of mental variation of power and refinement. The brilliant silvery light came from the well-balanced and refined brain; while those who were gross and low, emitted a more sombre current of electric fluid.

But the sphere of my vision now began to widen. My mental power of penetration was no longer subject to the laws of density; all the surrounding objects appeared as transparencies. Nature's spacious cabinet was thrown open to me; and for a while I imagined that I alone was drinking in the beauties of this magnificent banquet. But my conclusions were incorrect, for while I was mentally analyzing the distinctly visible properties of surrounding objects, I became suddenly conscious of the presence of other observers. These were forms of transcendent beauty. Their beauteous form emitted a ceaseless glow of fine, nervous light. I soon discovered that they were devoid of physical forms, and somehow my mind was impressed with the idea that I was in the presence of purely spiritual beings, towards whom I felt an irresistible attraction.

Words utterly fail to delineate the gorgeous panorama now unfolded to my expanded vision. I saw that each object was beautifully and distinctly surrounded by an atmosphere of life; and instinctively I recognized in this phenomena the wonderful mystery of the law of sympathy and attraction. I saw that everything in nature was arranged and located in accordance with this universal law; that it was the fundamental principle of sympathetic relation. The connecting link between objects, the invisible operation of the universal law of change. Throughout the universe I saw that there was a generous commingling of magnetic emanation; and thus the grand secret of affinity was brought before my mental vision. It is impossible for me to detail all the impressions I received, and emotions I experienced on this occasion of my first introduction into a clairvoyant perception of Nature. Nor can I portray the harmonious beauties that I witnessed, while among the dwellers of the fadeless summer-land. For, though I was conscious of their presence, I was aware of a strong attraction to earth life; and that this attraction held me from mingling with them freely.

In this vision I saw, by the penetrating power of a freed spirit, everything just as we will all see them after we pass away from the visible body at physical death.

Suddenly I was conscious that the extended scope of my vision was undergoing rapid contraction. The beautiful magnetic illumination swiftly faded; and soon I could only discern, as before, the magnetic condition of those in the room; and at last even this was lost. For a moment everything was shrouded in impenetrable darkness, which on being lifted, I found myself in a state of complete physical consciousness. My senses—the natural windows of my soul—were restored to their natural power, my organs of sight were unsealed, and the familiar light once more greeted my vision. Again I could hear the familiar voices of friends around.

During this condition of clairvoyance, I had unconsciously changed my position, and on my return to sensorial life, I found myself standing at the window gazing out into the darkness. As I turned and looked upon the circle of familiar friends, I saw that their countenances were expressive of intense wonder. My kind-hearted mother, who could not comprehend the philosophy of these strange spells, I saw had been weeping; and even others displayed feelings of horror. But on becoming convinced that I had returned to consciousness, this dread was supplanted by a feeling of anxiety to learn what I had witnessed, and and what were my sensations during my mental absence.

I gave my auditors but little satisfaction in answer to their anxious inquiries; for I felt then utterly incapable of portraying my sensations and impressions. So begging to be excused, I hurried away to the retirement of my own room to contemplate in solitude the mystic scenes of the night. Well do I remember my reflections on that memorable night. Vainly I strove to analyze and comprehend the mysterious cause of the beautiful phenomena I had experienced. Was it the result of a natural law, or a dream? An imaginary display, or a philosophical reality? In my own mind, there was an inspired thought which assured me that it was an important and beautiful truth—a philosophical reality, freighted with valuable consequences to mortals in their primary condition. I saw in this mysterious power of mental expansion a key that would ultimately unlock the invisible store-house of nature—filled, as it was, with rich treasures of mystic beauty—and bring to light the secret workings of invisible matter, and point out the connection between heaven and earth; that, aided by this beautiful and providential agency, man in his rudimental life would ultimately have clearer conceptions of the infinite.

CHAPTER VI.

MISUNDERSTANDING OF MY GIFTS.

ON THE morning following the events narrated in the last Chapter, I discovered, on entering the room, where the family had congregated, that their thoughts were still connected with the strange phenomena of the last night. Evidently it was something beyond their ready comprehension, a sort of magnetic or mesmeric mystery they had not expected to witness in connection with my mediumistic powers. Hence, being unexpected and unaccountable, their inferences were freighted with possible consequences of personal evil. From a look of extreme languor, mingled with an expression of sadness, apparent on the sympathetic countenance of my mother I conjectured that she had passed a night of mental trouble, arising from probable prospects that I had received physical or mental injuries. But the old look of mental quiet returned, when on enquiry, they found that I had suffered neither of these dreaded calamities. By request, I now explained my sensation and delineated in a bungling manner the wonders I had discovered, while in this mysterious condition of mental expansion. On finishing my rehearsal my father positively asserted that I had been in the realms of spirits; substantiating his conclusion by quotations of sundry similitudes from the experience of other mediums. Becoming elated over his visionary and sanguine anticipations of what my powers would ultimately be, he prophecied that at no distant day he should see me occupying the rostrum as a medium of superior knowledge. His reading had gave him an insight into many of the mysteries of clairvoyance which to my mind were perfectly incomprehensible. I could form no connection between these peculiar mental gifts and the exalted position of an expounder of the mysteries of nature. Hence, I could not help smiling at what appeared the effects of thoughtless enthusiasm, or groundless imagination.

From this time forward our mediumistic experiments were frequent and successful. For, like the poet, who awoke from his slumbers to find himself famous, I, since my mysterious sleep, had become not exactly famous, but notorious, for my popularity had not kept pace with my notoriety. Almost every night our meetings were thronged by the marvel-loving members of our immediate community, who came for the sole purpose of witnessing the demonstration and receiving individual tests. A few came with honest purposes and a sincere desire to intelligently test the phenomena; but by far the greater portion had no other object in view than a morbid desire to satisfy a fondness for whatever savored of supernaturalism. At times this latter class appeared to be actuated by ludicrous and absurd ideas of spirit power, which was either the result of ignorance or malicious design to appropriate a failure to accomplish miraculous and impossible tests, to their small stock of false arguments, to be used against the possible facts of the phenomena.

I was, by this class of investigators, continually annoyed by inconsistent and unanswerable questions; of which the following are but a partial list, the absurdity of which are plainly evident. "Could I, or the controlling power, reveal the future?" "Were they (the questioners) going to succeed in this or that undertaking?" If I make such an investment will I succeed?" "Could I turn water into wine, or discover hidden treasures?" "Could I transmute sordid metals into refined gold?" These were a few of the inconsistent queries of the penurious and worldly minded class.

Bible fanatics had a different set of equally unanswerable queries: "Could I tell when the world would come to an end?" "Were they (the questioners) to be saved in the day of judgement?" "Was heaven a city with streets of gold?" "Where was the grave of Moses?" and so on to an almost unlimited extent. Still another class, consisting of beardless boys and simpering misses, with old maids, and bachelors on the shady side of life, who were extremely anxious to know what were their matrimonial prospects.

Of course all these questioners went away dissatisfied, and instead of getting answers to their foolish queries would receive some revelation of the mysteries of life, whereupon they would announce to their friends that I could do no more than others. Still there was another class of investigators, which, though they displayed more intelligence, were none the less inconsistent; of which the following account of my experience, with a pompous old gentleman, furnishes a very good example.

This particular individual was one of that class who are naturally, or by force of habit, opponents. He gave me to understand that he designed to impartially test this modern spiritualism. Said he, "I design to put you, or the spirits, or whatever power controlls you, to a fair trial, and if you, or whatever the power is, fails to accomplish the tests imposed, I shall feel it my duty to publicly expose you." Supposing his investigation would be intelligently and honorably conducted, and impartially considered, on principles of reason and justice, I replied, "that all I desired was a fair test, and an honest exposition, and no more."

Confident of my powers, I gave way to the influence, and the controlling power signified by writing a willingness to render practical elucidation of spirit existence and power. Immediately various voluntary and marvelous tests were given. My hands were thrust into the candle flame and held there long enough to have crisped the flesh to the bone if they had not been protected by some invisible and mysterious means. The stand was moved back and forth across the room without any visible assistance and with only the tips of my fingers resting upon it. Certain articles were held on an inclined plain in direct opposition to the natural laws of gravitation, without visible support. Raps were produced with undeniable distinction in various parts of the room; while both mental and oral questions were answered with almost invarible correctness. All who witnessed the demonstrations on this occasion, with the single exception of this individual, admitted themselves satisfied that there was no imposition practiced, and that they were convinced that I was the medium of some foreign cause. Even he admitted that what he had witnessed was truly marvelous. Still being incredulous he diverged from honest, intelligent investigation in inconsistency. The most ulterior proof possible would only be acceptable and convincing. A friend of his, who he stated was a firm spiritualist, had informed him that he had known the spirits, through Mr. Slade, a highly developed medium, to ring bells and play on musical instruments without the application of any visible means; with various other, to use his own mode of expression, "miraculous feats." "Now," continued he, "if the spirits had once done these things, and he did not doubt the affirmation of his friend, hence believed they had, they could repeat the performance, and if it could be done through *Mr. Slade*, he could not see why the same thing could not be accomplished through me." No sooner had he completed this highly unphilosophical demand, than I was influenced to write the following, which I insert from memory. The phraseology may differ from the original, but the subject matter is intact. I insert it for the benefit of developing mediums, who, as in my case, may be tormented by similar inconsistent and incredulous investigators; and for those who may indulge the same absurd ideas of spirit or medial power.

"Every element of creation is subject to limit. Human beings, in their rudimental condition or earth life, are subject to this inevitable principle of limitation of power; which limitation is, in view of the law of progression, largely the result of intellectual capacity; for it is undeniable that variation in mental or intellectual capacity is the primary cause of the manifest diversity of powers to produce effects. Hence, what is possible to one man is impossible to another, different in power. Spirits not being infinite are subject to this same law. Therefore, what one spirit can accomplish may become, by this fact, of limitation an impossible feat to another.

The influencing powers now present are capable of perverting the natural tendencies of things, to a certain limited extent, through this medium. They can hold bodies of certain weight in opposition to the natural law of gravitation; they can also move the table or stand; but because they could move these, it was inconsistent to suppose that they could by the same means, move the house in which we were seated from

from its foundation. Would the questioner suppose it consistent to believe that, because one individual could just lift a body of certain weight, that a weaker one could accomplish the same feat? Or because an an electric battery, of given power, was capable of transmitting intelligence along a telegraph wire a thousand miles and no more, did it follow that one of half the power could be expected to do the same? Was it not consistent to suppose that the power to perform should in all cases be equal to the task imposed? Certainly, this principle was undeniable in regard to finite beings of earth and it is equally applicable to spirits; for spirits are not infinite. There is, nor can there be, in any stage of existence, but one infinite power.

Therefore, in view of this limitation of power among spirits, it must be readily perceived that those who understand the law and can control the means, are able to accomplish more wonderful feats than those who are ignorant of the principles and the means to be employed. Could it be reasonably expected that a person unskilled in music could perform on a musical instrument equal to a proficient? Certain spirits, who were acquainted with the art, and understood the means to be employed, could influence Mr. Slade, and through him as a medium, accomplish the wonderful feat of ringing bells and playing on musical instruments without visible application of power. But it did not necessarily follow that the spirits influencing this medium, who were ignorant of music and the means to produce the phenomena, could do the same."

Notwithstanding the plain, simple logic of this explanation, or rather excuse, this pompous and malicious investigator publicly pronounced me an impostor. But, while he proclaimed my inability to accomplish his imposed tests, he studiously withheld my reasons for not doing them from the public. Thus being without the shield of popularity I became the target of ignorant and malicious fanatics, subject to continual misrepresentation. I was looked upon by some as an impostor, by others as insane. But in spite of all this fanatical and bigoted array of opposition, there was a few honest, intelligent men and women, who nobly cheered me on, confident that I would, with unseen aids, outride the storms of private scandal and public ridicule.

CHAPTER VII.

DOUBTS AND MISGIVINGS WHY I WAS DIFFERENT FROM OTHERS.

ABOUT the first of September, 1853, occurred a perfectly natural, though memorable event of my life. I was now nineteen, consequently began to experience an irrepressible desire for conjugal happiness and enjoyment. For once, the old proverb that "true love never runs smooth," was practically denied, for my matrimonial projects were in every respect satisfactorily a success. I sought, and found congeniality of sentiment. Wealth, or worldly possessions, either real or prospective, were unconsidered; our union was founded upon the pure principles of reciprocal affection. Love, unsophisticated and pure, was alone the mystic tie that bound our hearts in wedded unison.

Not long after our marriage, my wife found on trial that she was, like myself, susceptible of mesmeric psychological influence. This discovery was to me a source of some little satisfaction; for I now had the means of witnessing the external appearances of this strange, mystic phenomena. On the other hand, the discovery was a source of considerable domestic concern, for I saw, with considerable anxiety, that there was probable danger that we might become so enthralled, or rather enveloped, in the mystic folds of an apparently uncontrollable magnetic power as to cause difficulty in future extrication. This (perfectly groundless) fear was, in part the result of my own ignorance, and in part arose from the harpings of equally ignorant persons, who being interested in our welfare, confidently asserted that these psychological influences would prove injurious to us both, and ultimately ruin our health. The bare prospect of such a calamity was sufficient to arouse the deepest anxiety; for health was the foundation of our happiness,—aye, more than that, in my case health was the bank from which I drew means of subsistence; for not being blessed with wealth, all my comforts, and even necessities, were the direct proceeds of manual toil. Hence, health adequate to labor was an absolute necessity of my life.

We often entered into private conference and discussed the prospect of our unknown and prospectively mysterious future. In these discussions the subject of this supposed spirit power, and the possible influence it might have on our happiness, was ever an unsettled theme. Would we be benefitted thereby, or would it lead to infamy and woe, were our oft-repeated queries. The world, the Church, and our own ignorance pointed to the darker ultimate; but in the midst of these misgivings, there was a mysterious something which whispered to our hearts that all would yet be radiant with the brightness of tranquil peace, and this undefinable something irresistibly impelled us on toward a more perfect magnetic development. When I gave way to these latter mysterious promptings, a feeling of peaceful tranquility would magically dispel the dark forbodings of my mind, and serene enjoyment would arise to prospective view.

But for all this, I could not enter into any specified ideas of what my future would be. I was blindly laboring up the steep slopes of the, to me, unexplored mountain of usefulness. I did not experience any sanguine anticipations of future renown. I was utterly devoid of ambitious desires to gain popular eminence. In short, I experienced a heart-felt and decided objection to being considered anything more than an ordinary person. Hence, I had no sympathy for the visionary prospects of notoriety, or even usefulness, over which my friends, and particularly my father, had manifested extraordinary anticipations. In view of my natural diffidence, combined with an intelligent appreciation of the fact that I was ignorant of even the simplest rules of public elocution, I made a firm resolve that nothing should induce me to appear as a public speaker. But, like many another, I found that I was emphatically a creature of circumstances, and fully recognized the truthfulness of Shakespeare's oft-quoted and oft-verified lines, that

"Fate would shape our ends, rough hew them as we may."

At this time my influence had assumed a peculiar

phase—being a condition of psychological somnolence. When in this condition, I was devoid of sensorial feeling or mental ability. I was like a machine or "spout" through which flowed a stream of refined intelligence, emanating from a foreign source. All my muscular movements were caused by the same mysterious agency, from whence came the intelligence. My language was not my own, and was generally more refined and diversified than I was, when myself, capable of using. In short, I was, when in this condition of somnolence, like one under narcotic influence; for though I was a living, moving being, I was devoid of mental independence or individuality, and like the somnambulist, I was unconscious of, and irresponsible for my acts or words.

One evening, on my being relieved from one of these somnambulic states, my father informed me that on this occasion I had been influenced by a *new spirit*, and that he (the spirit) had through me delivered an excellent discourse upon the philosophy of spirit intercourse; and so, continued my elated progenitor, you see my prophesy is being verified; for the controlling power has through you announced that he would dictate a public discourse on the benefits of spiritualism, to be delivered at the school-house on the coming Sabbath; and confident that you would consent, I have authorized those who were present to circulate the appointment.

Here was a pretty condition of affairs. I was unwittingly going to be forced to do what I had, in my own mind, firmly resolved that I would not; and in a moment of exasperation I told my sanguine, though well-meaning father that I would not fill the appointment. That night, in the quiet of my own room, I felt truly despondent. Why, thought I, am I forced to be the unwilling medium of a, to me, incomprehensible power of intelligence? I had no remembrance when awake of what I had seen or said when in this mystic slumber. Could I have been priveleged to have retained in memory those words which my friends told me were vehicles of deep scientific truth, I should have experienced no dread, nor sadness, such as now depressed my mind; but should have looked upon this strange gift with deepest feelings of gratitude. But as it was, I was afflicted with torturing misgivings. I had no personal knowledge of my somnambnlic powers. My friends told me that on this occasion I had been the medium of a rich oratorical and scientific discourse, and that I had handled the subject with all the ability of a studied philosopher. But I saw that my friends were wrought up to the highest pitch of enthusiasm, hence I could not consider them as competent judges. What to do I knewnot. Should I fill the appointment, and publicly risk my reputation, or should I firmly adhere to my hastily expressed determination not to speak, and thus trample upon the feelings of my father and friends? To whom could I apply for counsel? Of all those who were present, and heard this last manifestation, there was only one whom I dare trust as a critic, and I now resolved that

I would gain his honest opinion in regard to my oratorical abilities, when under influence; furthermore, I resolved that I would be entirely controlled by his decision.

On the following morning I laid the matter before this friend. I gave him to understand that I desired a plain, honest, impartial criticism of my mediumistic abilities for public speaking, and if he thought the discourse to which he had listened was sufficiently perfect in delivery, sound in reason and philosophy to withstand the criticisms of the learned. I told him I was anxious to please my friends, but did not desire by doing so to risk my reputation by making a ridiculous failure. In answer to these inquiries, he told me that my discourse of the night before was an extraordinary manifestation of intelligence; that the subject chosen was scientifically discussed; that my reasoning were deep and powerful, and unexceptionable. My language was good, the only defect being an occasional deviation from modern rules of grammar and orthœpy. He advised me by all means to fill the appointment. "Show to the world," said he, "that you are honestly, and sincerely in earnest; that you are the medium of a high order of intelligence, and I assure you that you will win the respect of even sceptics and unbelievers; and by such a course your friends will be bound to sustain you."

This conversation had a tendency to revive my spirits, and in the course of the day I informed my father that I had reconsidered my hasty conclusion, and that I had finally concluded to deliver the promised lecture; adding that I did not wish to again be inveigled into another such predicament.

The day on which I was to fulfill my promise had at length arrived. My present recollection of that first appearance in public is extremely vivid. On my arrival at the house, I found it already filled with an intelligent audience, who eyed me sharply as I wended my way through the crowded aisle toward the speaker's stand. 'Twas a new and painful trial for me, presenting myself thus, blushing with timidity and reservation, before a strange and heterogenous assembly, two-thirds of whom I was confident had no other motive for being present than to gratify curiosity, or criticise my endeavors. It is impossible for me to define my impressions, as I timidly raised my eyes and met their sharp, concentrated gaze. Alas! thought I, what would be my feelings if I should fail? I would become a scoff. I had no idea what I was going to do; all depended upon the mystic powers by which I was controlled. But the throng around me would attribute a failure to me alone.

Happily, while I was suffering from this painful embarrassment, I began to feel the precursory omens prognostic of approaching unconsciousness, gradually overcoming my sensorial powers of mind, and in a few moments I was totally oblivious of my surroundings. I have no personal remembrance of what transpired during the two hours I was in this unconscious state of somnambulism. But on my return to sensorial life, I saw a look of heart-felt satisfaction resting on the countenances of my friends, and I further saw that those whom I felt were opposers appeared thoughtful and perplexed; and from these omens, I judged that my endeavors had been a success. The meeting was closed by some explanatory remarks concerning the phenomena, by my father and others. To the most of the assembly the proceedings were a complete mystery, as well as novelty. All who were personally acquainted with me, positively knew that the discourse was far beyond my natural abilities ; hence, many who had before disbelieved in the possibility of my receiving assistance from any foreign source, were literally forced to admit the fact that I was a medium on this occasion. I had been a mystery before, I was now a marvelous person. The old cry of "Humbug," would no longer keep people from investigating. My position was now unimpeachable ; and though I was subject to gross misrepresentations, and was a target for the hot-shot of ignorant fanatics, who would believe only what St. Paul, or some other saint had pronounced true, I had the satisfaction of knowing that I was slowly but surely gaining in popular estimation. People began to search into the mystery of these strange manifestations, and the deeper they searched, the more proof did they find that the controlling power emanated from spirits. In fact, it was the only satisfactory solution of the phenomena, and many avowed their belief to be in accordance with this hypothesis—very much to the alarm of those who knew naught, nor dare not think of the mysteries of God's law beyond what he had revealed in his divine word.

CHAPTER VIII.

DIFFERENT VIEWS OF SPIRITUALISM.—WHAT IT IS.

"Reason cannot know,
What sense can neither feel nor thought conceive,
There is delusion in the world,—and woe,
And fear, and pain."

DURING these early stages of spirit manifestation, the phenomena had received but very little philosophical investigation; and a large portion who admitted themselves believers of the doctrine of spiritualism, clothed their ideas with the mystery of supernaturalism. Many claimed this modern spirit intercourse to be one of the special providences of God, a second coming of the Mesiah, or special re-inauguration of a defunct or suspended privilege formerly enjoyed and practiced by ancient seers and prophets. Even writers, what few there were who dared to treat the subject favorably, clothed their erudition in the cabalistic mysteries characteristic of ancient astrology and prophecy. Highly visionary productions, redundant with inconsistent and never-to-be-realized prophecies, mingled with a moity of uncertain and impracticle probabilities, were published to the world as bona fide elucidation of the phenomena, and over all was thrown a garb of semi religion. Honest matter-of-fact investigators, who, tired of mystery and bigotry, were in search of more practical theories, and who candidly believed there were scientific truths humanizing in their influence, in spiritualism, were retarded in giving their honest convictions publicity, simply because they could not affiliate their opinions with the nonsensical productions of these sanguine and insanely fanatical visionists.

Being that I was closely connected with the phenomena as a medium, I took more than ordinary interest in the subject; and hence, in order that I might have the benefit of some studied exposition and explanation, I possessed myself of various works purporting to scientificly solve the mystery and depict the ultimate or final perfection of, and benefit to be realized from this newly revived intercourse between disembodied spirits and man. But I must in candor admit that I arose from their perusal more ignorant and mystified than before. For to my practical mind their glorious ultimate appeared as a purely heterogeneous mixture of impossible theories and impracticable probabilities, utterly beyond the scope of reason, judgement, or good sense.

In my own mind I condemned these visionary fulminations, I looked upon spiritualism as a natural science, having no more connection with religion or supernaturalism than any other natural phenomena. My personal investigations had proven to my understanding that spirits laid claim to no infinite powers or God like infalability; their teachings were purely practical and designed immediate aggrandizement of the human family while in their rudimental state. They taught how to live instead of how to die, and how to arrive at the greatest amount of earthly happiness. Having by practical investigation arrived to the conclusion that spiritualism was a science, an operation of natural law, I considered it highly impracticable and injudicious for spiritualists to endeavor to overreach consistency by undertaking to unveil the incomprehensible future beyond actual powers of science to determine. Those conclusions I have ever retained, and I to-day believe that the phenomena of spiritualism, both in cause and effect, bears no more resemblance to religion, nor is it more infalible, than any other scientific operation of natural law. Hence, the sooner it is divested of all its hifalutin visionistic ingrediences, and supernatural appearances, the sooner will we reap practical benefits therefrom.

Having carefully contemplated the matter and studied the phenomena from a practical standpoint, and from experience, I concluded to continue my mediumistic career in a sincere belief that it would sometime result in something beneficial. Though what that something was I had not the remotest idea. I was dissatisfied with all my former mediumistic positions. As a test medium I only appealed to the minds of the curious who were ever on the alert for possible deception. The position of a lecturer I perfectly abhorred. Theories were too unstable, and though they might be logically established beyond refutation, still they were often impracticable, and that simple fact was enough to completely destroy the charm of a public life as a lecturer. But notwithstanding my opposition to this latter position, I was continually harrassed by my friends, who were determined that I should continue my lectures. My former success had increased their ardor. Becoming at last tired of their ceaseless importunities, I, like the maid who married the man to get rid of him, consented to gratify their wishes. By this arrangement my father was greatly pleased. The acme of his ambition was to see me occupying the position of lecturer. Spiritualism had become with him almost a hobby, and it was his inevitable topic of conversation; and these public lectures being, as they were, conducted on the "free discussion" principle, were productive of chances for him to freely indulge his passionate fondness for argument. During these lectures I was subjected to the closest investigation. I unconsciously waged war against many of the established and fundamental principles of the orthodox world; and, as free discussion was the order, I was opposed both by the learned and ignorant, and for real and often imaginary opposition to their theories. That is I was often called to account for what my auditors ignorantly supposed to be anti-orthodox positions, but which in reality were not.

I do not doubt but these lectures were productive of some good, inasmuch as they were well attended by a truth seeking and truth loving portion of the community. They certainly inculcated a liberal sort of doctrine, and their whole tenor was in opposition to that heir-loom of heathenism, and catholic religion, superstition. During these lectures I found that ignorance was man's strongest enemy, and the prime cause of his greatest misfortunes. Superstition was the legitimate offspring of this tyranical monster; and that much of the so-called orthodoxical and religious enthusiasm, was the direct result of this remnant of heathenism. I found that the terms "superstition" and "religion" were synomious to a certain extent. With a large portion to be religious, was in their estimation to occupy a position *above the world*, and put their trust in whatsoever appeared as supernatural, or in other words, their ignorance irresistibly impelled them to doubt the known and rely confidingly upon the incomprehensible. This class of superstitious religionists were continually tormented by vague and undefined ideas, or sort of half belief in the existence of such supernatural personages as ghosts, witches, imps, etc., who they vaguely supposed might exert more or less influence on the character and action of human beings. This class confidently believed that I was the victim of impish incantation; and I do not doubt but what many came to see me in the honest expectation of seeing a vertable habitant of the other world, brought forth by some satanic power I was supposed to possess. Had I possessed the power many supposed I did, I should have rapidly converted to spiritualism many of the most enthusiastic religionists of the country; for they were so wrapped up in superstition as to make it impossible for them to doubt the incomprehensible. Their faith in the supernatural was supported by irresistable evidence. They saw no divinity in any comprehensive truth. So long as spirit existence was incomprehensible, or only substantiated by mysterious assertions found in the Bible, they were faithful adherents to the doctrine. But they strenuously opposed any philosophical corroboration of this fact.

They expected to find me the advocate of the mysterious, they supposed I would naturally pander to their fondness for the supernatural by conjuring from their graves the ghosts of defunct mortality. Hence, when they found that I opposed superstition in every form, even grappling with their cherished doctrines of religious faith, by ignoring the unnatural and incomprehensible, by reducing everything to a comprehensive standard, they made me the victim of their religious anathemas, and with a spirit of zealous indignation, branded me as an infidel, as an opposer of religion, and defamer of God's written law.

This class of individuals were the victims of ignorance, who mistook Pagan superstition for pure religion, and their conduct went far to establish the universally conceded fact that the possession of knowledge makes all the difference there is between the religious opinions of the people of the nineteenth century and those of the days of Pagan Rome.

It is an undeniable fact that every ordinary mind is superstitious, unless it be refined and exalted by education. Hence, education is as much the standard of religion as morality.

But the views which I then advocated were firmly opposed by all classes of religionists. My principles were far too liberal for Christians who desired more fancy and less facts, more mystery and less philosophy; they could not brook the idea of reducing the mysterious probability of future existence to a plain and comprehensive standard of reality, nothing could induce them, no matter how sensible or philosophical the opposing proof might be, to give up their pet belief in a literal new Jerusalem, with streets of gold, or the great white throne, around which would be gathered the nations of the earth, singing the song of hozanna through all eternity. I was not opposed for teaching immorality, no one ever accused me of giving utterance to a single immoral sentence. But I opposed their dearly cherished "superstition," sifted from the good this remnant of the Pagan eras, thereby reducing their religions to a position more practical, and more clearly defined than their natural regard for the supernatural could be brought to endorse.

Of course this position was not universal. Many who listened to these discourses were led to consider my position as reasonable and philosophical. Some who had been life-long religionists endeavored to introduce some of the liberal principles I advocated into their every-day life, for which noble acts they received speedy condemnation from the church. The fact that I was a medium of some foreign intelligence was now fully substantiated; no one longer pretended to deny the hypothesis, and from this time forth I was rid of the obnoxious appellation of "humbug."

During the time I was engaged in these lectures a new phase of mediumistic power was introduced. Heretofore I had been influenced by spirits who manifested themselves either by physical tests or theoretical discussion. But I was now occasionally controlled by what purported to be the spirit of an Indian doctor. My other gifts or manifestations of spirit phenomena had been the means of gaining for me a position of notoriety; but this new phase was a stepping stone to popular esteem, and by it all my plans of life were destined to be completely revolutionized. Judging from the enthusiasm of my friends, and my rapidly increasing popularity, it was evident that these manifestations were far more wonderful than any of my preceding demonstrations. All were astonished at my unerring accuracy in delineations of disease; there was no chance for deception. Persons who came for examination invariably went away satisfied, and though skeptics tried by various means to disprove my magnetic abilities or clairvoyant powers, they could not turn the incoming tide of intelligent favor which was fast swallowing up their ill-conceived efforts to fasten on me the brand of "studied deception." It was impossible to make those who had tested this new power believe themselves deceived, or that my delineations were the result of guess work.

CHAPTER IX.

A CHAPTER OF MYSTERIES.

"I am not
What I seem; nor yet a hypocrite,
But what I am I hardly know."

I WAS now living a wonderful two-fold daily life, a sort of double existence. The boundary line which divided my common from my superior condition, was sharply defined. Ordinarily I was a shy, uneducated, hard working mechanic; but when in my superior or psychological condition, I became a remarkable intellectual prodogy. By the assistance of this new phase of psychological power I was endowed with marvelous abilities. I could delineate with almost unerring accuracy, the physical feeling of every applicant. Could locate and define every pain human flesh was heir to. The human organism became as an open book; and by means of this clairvoyant inspection I ascertained that disease was a want of equilibrium in the circulation of the vitalic principles. That there was either an *excess* in some organ or locality, or else a deficiency. I found that the result of the former was what was termed *acute* or inflammatory disease, while the latter derangement resulted in chronic or surreptitious complaints, and that each form required very different treatment from the other. I saw that one cause often produced various effects, and *vice versa*, that one effect was the result of widely different causes. For instance, I discovered that one type of fever, though alike in outward appearance, in different individuals, was hardly ever the result of the same cause. I saw the folly of uniformity of treatment, for it was evident to my clairvoyant understanding that in order to permanently remove the effect the cause must be eradicated; and that where the effect was the result of many different causes, that there must necessarily be a difference in treatment to effect a removal of the cause and create a cure. But what was most remarkable and beautiful was the fact that, while in my clairvoyant condition I seemed to be a sort of connecting link between the patient's disease and nature's remedy. For each visceral or organic deficiency in the human structure, I instinctively perceived a corresponding agent of gratification or restitution. Even for functional, nervous, or muscular necessities, I could easily discover an appropriate and adequate supply. By means of this wonderful power of vision I could look through space directly into nature's laboratory, or even into medical establishments, and discover the existence of these various agents or remedies for disease. By these means of observation I acquired the common (and even Greek and Latin) names of various medicines; and also, of many parts of the human structure. These wonderful powers greatly astounded the people, and myself not less when not clairvoyant; for even I had to rely solely upon hearsay and gossip for information in regard to my own acts.

The secret of my medical success is simply the bringing together of specific medicines to supply a philosophical demand, or to equalize the unballanced vitalic principle. And yet during the first years of my medical experience I could not give a satisfactory solution of my own method. In fact I did not comprehend the full import of my own perception well enough to harmonize their opposites, or form pefect connection between disease and nature's remedies. The reason was I had not yet reached my present superior condition, and as I was imperfectly developed as a clairvoyant the controlling power was unable to assume complete control of my organism. Practice is as much a ncessity in clairvoyant practice as any other branch of progressive science.

No sooner had it become noised about that I could locate diseases, describe the feelings of patients, and analyze and apply curative agencies, than my heretofore quiet home became a central place of attraction for the afflicted. People suffering from all conceivable types of physical maladies, came to listen to my delineation of their various grievances and learn if I could discover in nature's extensive laboratory a healing balm for their ills. Many who came before me had been given up by the faculty and their disciples as incurable, but they did not doubt but what a person of my wonderful abilities could cure them, and by supernatural power snatch them from even the closing jaws of death.

Hence, in the very outset of my career as a practical physician, I was put to the severest test. No one denied but my diagnosis of disease was invariably correct, but my abilities to cure were, to say the least, doubtful; and, therefore, the effect of my prescriptions were narrowly watched. Probably one reason for this close scrutiny was owing to my aptness to prescribe unheard of remedies; and another to the fact that I went in opposition to scholastic precedent; in many instances my prescriptions were directly opposed to long standing rules of medical practice. For reasons before mentioned, I utterly ignored all principles of uniformity of practice. I applied my powers for the removal of the cause, other practitioners sought to move the effect, and therein was the reason for our variance.

My first case was my brother's little child, who had from her birth been afflicted with a scrofulous humor of the blood; which at this time, had resulted in an obnoxious and highly dangerous affection of the head and oflactory membranes and occult nerves. Different physicians had been successively baffled in their attempt to furnish even the slightest relief. Old women of medical proclivities and pretentions, pronounced her incurable. But contrary to the belief of scholarly practitioners or the assertion of old women, my prescriptions proved highly useful, and in due course of time, by careful treatment, the supposed incurable child was restored to excellent health.

From that time my position as a practical physician was fully established and recognized by a large portion of the surrounding community. Many placed the most implicit confidence in my abilities, which confidence, as I added each day new laurels to my mystic fame, grew into admiration. But my fame as a physician was subject to inconceivable exageration, and occasionally an applicant would come before me who, in consequence of exagerated rumors, honestly supposed me capable of miraculous deeds. On one occasion, I remember, an ignorant Hibernian, a victim of Catholic superstition, came to get me to go and raise his " did mither who was just then died, from the grave." This victim of superstition conscientiously believed I had the power of literally raising the dead ;" and though he was an extreme he was hardly an exception, for there was many more intelligent persons who thought me capable of performing wondorful and supernatural feats of wizzard mystery.

But even during this time, I occasionally experienced feelings of uncertainty and doubts of the actual value and usefulness of my strange gifts; and these misgivings served to dampen that aspiration which is natural to youth. Had it not been for my father and the influence of admiring friends, I think my dreamy and unambitious mind would have led me to have ignored my powers. But day by day there was imperceptibly woven a golden web of sympathetic interest and strange mystery, which brought me in contact with numerous intelligent admirers, persons of all degrees of intelligence, who valued my rare gifts, and extolled in unmeasured terms the good I was doing; yet I remained in spirit unmoved and strictly dispassionate. I experienced no pride, no vanity, no ambition for distinction, no fondness for power, no desire for wealth, no aspiration for education, no sensation of vaunting self-importance, or vanity of position. Calmly the unseen current of my dispassionate soul moved down the stream of life; from hour to hour, from day to day, from week to week, I contentedly traveled on without realizing that I was taking a single progressive step toward a greater and purer psyshological development. Now I toiled and labored at my mechanical pursuit for daily bread; and then, at the call of the afflicted, I would suffer myself to pass into a state of unconsciousness and examine the present or absent sick. On being relieved I would go out and get a breath of fresh air and return to my labor. Thus for months I dwelt in this uncertain physical valley, where a gray haze pervaded and bedimed every intellectual object, giving a doubtful appearance to my immediate future; and yet I was unconsciously climbing up the mountain of human usefulness.

Each day was a literal repetition of the preceding. The sick came from all directions; poor diseased humanity, aching, groaning, limping, coughing, dying.

My house was filled to excess; and such was the demand upon my time that I was forced to neglect my legitimate occupation ; and my external life was mainly spent in unconscious slumber.

I could find no time to continue my lectures ; and in consequence my father became petulent and dissatisfied. His argumentive spirit saw no beauty in anything aside from theory. But the people demanded physical not intellectual assistance; therefore, he was forced to assume a bearing of individual satisfaction, which when he saw my rapid strides toward popularity became a reality, and in due course of time he became my heartiest supporter.

The reader is not to infer from the above record that my psychological career received universal approval, or that my popularity was unalloyed by opposition. Numerous and intelligent opposers, professional men and fashionables, hurled at me the hot shot of condemnation. The mysterious phenomena of which I was a medium served to excite the curiosity of the surface population. The heart of the monster ignorance, and the prejudice of gloomy religionists, was fully aroused. Denominations and individuals arrayed themselves against me, and in their blind zeal declared me possessed with the spirit of the " devil." They attributed even my most charitable deeds, my acts of healing and alleviation of human suffering to his satanic majesty, and pronounced them the result of a covert and malignant design.

But even these malicious attempts to bring me into disrepute, proved futile. There were many who had received personal proof of my abilities, and these were confident that they were not deceived, nor victims of satanic design, and these could not be induced to reiterate the cry of devil.

In order to make the mysterious phenomena of clairvoyance more comprehensive and plain to the mind of my readers, I will relate the manner and style of my influence. I was subject to two forms of clairvoyant control, which I will term independent and dependent clairvoyance. By becoming passive and turning my thoughts inwardly, so as to shut out of my mind the fleeting disturbances and interruptions of the outer world, I would pass readily into the former, or independent condition. At such times my mind was rendered incapable of controling the slightest muscle, or of realizing any physical sensation. I was utterly unconscious of any physical relation. I seemed to exist only in spirit, and that spirit seemed gifted with extraordinary powers; and as I have before stated, density was no opposition to vision. I saw things in reality as persons often imagine they do in dreams. If I was called upon to investigate a human organism I found them as transparent as glass is to the natural vision. I could view every separate organ, see the operation of every fluid, and easily discern the most trivial derangement. At first I supposed there was no limit to my visionistic powers, and that distance was no impediment; but I have since learned this supposition to be incorrect, but am unable to furnish any plausible reason for the fact, or even state the exact distance my clairvoyant power of discernment is able to extend. I only know that on some occasions I can wander farther away from actual physical locality than others; consequently I am inclined to the opinion that when in this condition I am subject to atmospheric relation like an electro-telegraph.

Some imagine that when in this condition that I am nearly infinite, that I have prophetic powers, that I am all-seeing, and all-knowing, and that there is nothing beyond my comprehension. This idea is not only absurd bnt emphatically erroneous. I can only discern actualities or bodies having tangible existence. Spirit, or more properly speaking the essence of mind, is as indiscernible to my clairvoyant power as to my natural sight. The organic gasses, or at least the finer portions of them, are totally invisible to my clairvoyant vision. In short, even as an independent clairvoyant, I am subject to the immutible law of limit. My powers of penetration, and my sense of observation, or vision, is simply the result of electric connection, between the object contemplated or subject of observation, and the inner sense of comprehension or sight. The connection is direct. The eye, the natural medium of sight, is for the time robbed of its employment. The philosophy of this electric connection will be found farther on under the head of "clairvoyant powers."

My dependent clairvoyant abilities differ widely from the independent. Under this influence I am like a spout through which flows a current of foreign intelligence. When in this condition I am like a somnambulic, perfectly unconscious. I am not only physically but mentally under magnetic control. I know nothing of my surroundings, nor do I retain any remembrance of my acts or sayings. It is when in this condition that what purports to be spirit communications are received. And most of my professional examinations of persons who are diseased are made while in this condition, and are, therefore, the result of observation foreign to myself. During the first years of my professional career these physical examinations purported to emanate from the spirit of an Indian physician, who gave his name as "Walapaca." But at the present time they are given by another representative of our red brethren, known by my numerous friends as "Owosso."

CHAPTER X.

MORE MYSTERIES.

The world is full of mystery—
Wild, weird, and wonderful.

NUMEROUS mysterious psychological occurrences, and almost supernatural incidents of wizzard manifestations, which have, from time to time, assumed extremely startling witch-like phases of demonstration, have occurred during my life. and are considered by many as incomprehensible marvelous elucidations of spirit power, and by others as the result of satanic agencies.

Leaving the reader to judge for themselves concerning the origin of these strange manifestations, I will proceed to relate a few of those which can be substantiated by living testimony. I will state, however, that I believe them to be the result of spirit electric power. But I am not inclined to venture any opinion in regard to the cause of these manifestations or their probable effect upon the morals of community. I only relate them because they appear to have a connection with my life, though I cannot say they have had any influence over my mind or acts. There is another reason for my giving them publicity, and that is to rob them of their false additions, exagerations, and mysterious ingredients, for like the "three black crows," they have, by frequent relation, grown to be stupendous accounts of hobgoblin mystery.

The first of these strange manifestations occurred during the third year of my mediumistic career. On the evening in question a company of my young friends had called upon me for an hours social conversation. Having exhausted the gossip of the neighborhood, some one proposed as a change of programme, to form a circle and see what manner of communication we could get from the spirit world. All readily consented to this proposition, and with the exception of a semi-idiotic young man, who was then in my employ, every individual of the company connected themselves with the circle. Manifestations of spirit presence was soon received, and for some time we indulged our fondness for the marvelous, by the not then unusual occupation of fortune telling. But even this sort of doubtful amusement did not satisfy our unreasonable desires for mystery. Some one formally asked the spirits if we could not receive a manfestation from the woman, or to use the common expression, the "Witch of Endor." This request was entirely a thoughtless one, and not an individual present had the remotest idea that it would be attended with any result whatever. Nor do I to-day believe that the manifestations then received emanated from the Witch of Endor, but from a combination of spirits, whose sentiments were congenial to our own. We were young and thoughtless; we desired weird and mysterious manifestations, and we got just what our thoughtless minds craved.

No sooner was the request made than a peculiar, and with the exception of myself and wife, startling sensation was experienced by every member of the circle. Our hands were pressed down upon the table with irresistible force. In vain we tried to wrench them from the vice-like grip of the unseen power. Each called upon the other for assistance; but all were alike powerless to render any aid. Soon the table began a rapid gyration around the room. No one had the power to resist, but all were involuntarily impelled to follow the senseless article of furniture in its fantastic perambulations. Now commenced a complication of weird manifestations. Chairs and other light articles of furniture were hurled hither and thither about the room with fierce velocity, and in close proximity to our unguarded craniums. In the midst of this wild turmoil the lights had become extinguished, leaving us enveloped in impenetrable darkness. Doors were opened and shut, and for a time it seemed as if the house would be rent to pieces and come crashing in upon us. The poor frightened half idiot, being the only person free, was swiftly hurrying from door to door in a vain endeavor to fly from the ghostly scene; but though not a door was fastened, still he was unable to leave the room. Loud raps were heard to issue from all parts of the room, and the window shook as if under the influence of an hurricane power. This very strange phenomena lasted for some twenty minutes, when, as sudden as the visitation came, as quick and noiseless it departed. An almost painful silence followed the abrupt withdrawal of the mysterious power, and for a while we stood where the influence had left us, a silent awe-struck group, in anticipation of a recurrence of the scene. But there was no farther demonstration given. A light revealed to us the most astonishing phase of the manifestation; we expected to find every article of furniture in a state of complete disorder; but you can imagine our consternation when on inspection we found that not an article appeared to have been disturbed. This fact completely bewildered our minds and gave rise to an unanswerable set of conjectures. Was it hallucination of mind? phantasm of brain? had our imagination conjured out of nothing all this wild turmoil? Or was it really a manifestation of witch powers? These were agitated but undecided queries with us. For certain reasons we agreed to keep silent about the visitation, and from that day to this the real facts were never known. But somehow strange stories were circulated, which, for a wonder, fell far short of the real facts in point of mystery.

This in one point was the most startling phase of spirit electric power I ever witnessed. I never before or since saw such a manifestation of apparent muscular strength. There were seven individuals held by magnetic power aside from the electric force used to produce the various other forms of demonstration. I never attached any merit to these wizard manifestations. They only appealed to a morbid desire for mystery; and had it been in my power I should have rid myself of them entirely, but for some unaccountable reason I have been, all through my psychological career, occasionally tormented by evil spirits, or by useless manifestations of spirit power, which while they have done no material damage to the cause have been a source of individual annoyance and false representations. These manifestations were mostly unsought, and would make their appearance when least expected. I have often been startled out of profound sleep by loud raps on my pillow; have had articles of furniture hurled at my head when quietly conversing on ordinary topics with friends, and on one occasion was driven out of my office and kept out all day by a bewitched counter-brush, which seemed bent on doing me personal injury. My home has always been a sort of depot of mystery, and looked upon by the superstitious as being haunted on account of these strange noises. Sometimes even the most trivial circumstance would be contorted into hobgoblin mystery. Many of these startling stories were sheer fabrication, and even those which had a foundation of truth were subject to stupendous exageration.

As a fair sample of this aptness to exagerate, I I will give the actual truth, and also the false report concerning what is known as the white mouse phenomena. The real facts of the case were these:

During the fall and winter of 1854 the inmates of my house were more or less annoyed by a strange and incomprehensible noise, which apparently emanated from some invisible agency. This noise was an apparent imitation of human singing or humming, in a low indistinct key. But the greatest peculiarity about it was the impossibility to locate the exact point from which the sound proceeded. At times it would appear to be in the most remote room of the house, then it would be suddenly heard in the midst of the company; again it would appear to issue from the clock, pantry, bureau drawers, and other strange parts. The rapidity of these changes was what made the phenomena so mysterious. For a long time the probable cause of this sound was a matter of conjecture. Many who heard them quoted them as spirit manifestations. The mystery was at last divulged One evening, while a party of young friends were present, a beautiful white mouse was seen to run across the floor and take refuge in the pantry. His beauty and novel appearance created a desire for his capture, and instantly the whole company gave chase. After considerable search he was brought to bey in one corner of the room, and just as his pursuers supposed his capture certain, he threw them off their guard by a free exhibition of his wonderful vocal powers. For a moment he gave utterance to the same humming music that had been so long a subject of mystery, then suddenly taking advantage of the spell his display had caused among his would-be captors, he succeeded in making good his escape. Nothing more was ever seen of the mouse, nor was the music ever after heard.

This mouse was certainly a wonderful creature, and was probably a member of some rare specie of the animal kingdom, His vocal powers were like those of the common tree-toad, naturally ventriloquent, which would account for the apparent rapid change of locality.

From this extremely trivial circumstance of the singing mouse, numerous phantom stories were circulated. The singing was purported to be an exact *fac simile* of the human voice; and it was even said that songs and hymns were sang in most beautiful style. The poor mouse was reported to be everywhere present and capable of going in and out of trunks and drawers, through the key-hole, and of doing a hundred other impossible feats. Even after the mouse was found to be the cause of the music, some of the more fanatical believers of spirit power, argued that it was a messenger sent by the spirits, but for what purpose it was sent, they were unable to determine. I always considered it as a natural phenomena, and I only speak of it to illustrate the tendency of the human mind to a belief in the marvelous. And I note as one of many similar instances which have occurred during my mediumistic career.

Probably the most apparently supernatural occurrence that has occurred in connection with my life is the child-crying phenomena of a more recent date.

This manifestation has occurred at different periods for several successive years, and thus far it has baffled the closest investigation. I first heard it shortly after my removal to my present place of business; at first it appeared to be confined to one of the lower apartments of the house, and sounded like the loud crying of a child in great distress. It has been as often heard in the day time as in the night; in fact there is no regularity of occurrence, nor no apparent choice of persons. Strangers have heard it and supposed it the actual crying of a living infant. More recently it has been heard in other parts of the house. No ghostly appearance of a child has ever been witnessed in connection with the sound. It is altogether an incomprehensible phenomena, and though there has been various conjectures as to the probable cause of the strange visitation, there has never been any plausible or rather practical solution of the affair, and at the present time it has ceased to even be a subject of wonder.

As I have said, these, with various other weird manifestations have, from time to time, unsought, appeared in connection with my other mediumistic powers. The question naturally arises in regard to the reason why these phenomena should manifest themselves at such unreasonable times and when least expected? The solution to this query is perfectly philosophical, and the reason for these unsought manifestations, (I refer to the phenomena of the raps and like manifestations) is because I am naturally and alternately powerfully surcharged with vital magnetism and vital electricity. Magnetism, which is positive, and electricity, which is negative, will at different times preponderate or assume the ascendency in my system. When vital electricity predominates the raps may be produced. At these times my system is like the electric power of the torpedo eel, and is capable of discharging a small volume or current of vital electricity, which, by coming in sudden contact with the electricity of the atmosphere, causes by concussion the phenomena of the raps. The phenomena of articles being thrown towards me is caused by a preponderence of vital magnetism in my system, aided by spirit power. The direction of these projectiles is almost invariably determined by my present electrical or magnetical condition. When the magnetical is in the ascendency their movements are toward myself; but when the electrical condition preponderates they are moved in an opposite direction, and their movement is caused by the power of confined vital electricity seeking its equilibrium in the external atmosphere. This phenomena is not entirely an unusual occurrence. There are many individuals who are effected in like manner; but by their similarity, it is evident that certain conditions of mind and body are necessary to produce the phenomena, and this fact explains why these mysterious manifestations are confined to certain persons and localities.

CHAPTER XI.

MY PROGRESS AS A PHYSICIAN.

FROM the date of my first clairvoyant examination it was evident—as I have before stated—that this peculiar magnetic gift was destined to completely revolutionize my supposed prospects of life. My clairvoyant examinations of the sick were gradually becoming more frequent, and as we had settled upon fee for that kind of professional service, correspondingly profitable. Applicants were daily becoming more numerous, until such was the demand upon my time that I found it impossible to give my attention to any other branch of business. My time was divided between the labor of preparing medical compounds and examination of new cases, and also an occasional sitting for the less beneficial purpose of furnishing tests for incredulous investigators. Internally there had dawned upon me clearer, brighter, truer prospects of life, but externally I remained dull-headed, mystified, and apprehensive. In the secret seclusion of internal thought, I felt the sacred influence of noble aspirations, and a calm confidence in the unknown future. But, owing to the advice and outspoken opprobrium of officious acquaintances, I was retarded from giving external expressions to my nobler aspirations. Subjected to the buffetings of an opinionating community, my daily life was far from cheerful. Some contended that these psychological visitations "would make me sick;" others, "that I would become crazy;" some told me I was a "fool," and others still looked upon me as a humbug—a cheat—an impostor. But the day had gone by for such inferences to disturb the equilibrium of my internal thought. Past experience had proven that my health was not endangered; nor could I discern any prognostication of probable insanity. Externally, I knew, there was a probable ground for the appellation of fool; but who, thought I, is competent to analyze my interior thoughts? Was not my fast increasing popularity a sufficient denial of the malicious accusation of imposition? Beside, had not my medical treatment proved a complete success, and a subject of wonder? Unsought testimonials began coming into my possession, sent as mementoes of heart-felt gratitude, from those who had been recipients of glorious benefits as the proceeds of my mystic power. Reason and philosophy were powerful champions of my peculiar gifts, and every day scientific research was revealing new proof, and destroying the argument of opposition. And so, relying upon the better promptings of my own internal thoughts, I continued to gradually ascend the rugged mountain of usefulness. A feeling of tranquility at this time pervaded my whole life. My mind was allowed to roam, free and untrammeled, through the Elysian fields of thought, and though my ideas were crude and uncertain, they were none the less pleasurable. New fields of usefulness were opening to view; my mind was undergoing a rapid change; formerly I had looked upon every occupation aside from manual toil, as effeminate, and beneath the dignity of muscular manhood. But now I recognized that I had a mission to perform—a mysterious psychological mission—of great practical worth to the human family. I was now happier than formerly, for I saw a work to do. In this mission of active effort I discovered a new significance in life. I found that the hitherto indefinable mystery of my life was capable of being the means of a degree of human happiness; and gladdened by these thoughts I felt my sympathies going out towards all the human race. In my own heart I resolved that the scoffs of the ignorant should no longer divert me from the path of apparent duty.

Let the reader now glide with me over twelve months of ceaseless, unvarying labor. During this time I spent from four to six hours per day in an unconscious condition of psychology. My house had been converted into a medical laboratory and dispensary; on every hand the olfactory organs of visitors would be greeted with the strong fragrance of medicinal preparations. Numerous employees were engaged in gathering from the garden of nature balms for human ills. Applicants were daily becoming more numerous, and the confidence of the public correspondingly firm. Professional opposers, finding that their anathemas could not beat back the incoming and fast increasing tide of popularity, looked on with sullen indifference. And thus, by simply following the recommendations of a well-earned reputation, I laid the foundation of future success as a practical physician.

Numerous invitations to visit other localities created a desire in the unstable mind of my father for a wider field of operations; and as I admitted him to act as adviser and general master of ceremonies, I at once agreed to go wherever his judgment might dictate. It was accordingly arranged that I should make periodical visits to various places along the line of the Michigan Southern and Northern Indiana R. R., and that on these visits my father should officiate as right-hand man. Our first halt was in the beautiful and picturesque city of Adrian. There we met a large circle of liberal minded, intelligent representatives of spiritual progress—noble men and women whose hearts were free from the confining power of limiting sectarianism—who received us as co-laborers in the cause of truth. Men of intelligence, though sceptics in belief, who visited us were astonished to find in me—a still bashful, awkward youth—such apparent depth of scientific knowledge; and many who had before conscientiously supposed me an impostor—a trickster—were forced to admit that their former suppositions were erroneous. Professional disciples of Esculapius were invited to test my medical abilities and myster-

4

ious knowledge of human anatomy. Triumphantly and calmly my unseen guide bore me through this ordeal of studied and intelligent investigation, and every day new accessions were added to our long list of admiring friends. For two weeks we lingered in in this atmosphere of appreciated fraternal love; and when we left we received the earnest God-speed of many cherished and unforgotten friends. We next visited Coldwater, White Pigeon, and several other places; and in each place we met with the same warm-hearted greeting and bestowal of fraternal friendship. By this trip numerous additions were made to our already long list of patients, and I found, on my return home, that it would be impossible for me to properly attend to the wants of numerous applicants. I was, therefore, forced to call upon the psychological assistance of my wife, who, the reader will remember, had sometime before been developed as a "dependant clairvoyant."

Personally, I was much benefited by this sojourn among strangers, as it gave me a chance of making a more comprehensive inspection of external life than I had ever before enjoyed. My knowledge of humanity in the aggregate was, in view of my life-long seclusion from the world, extremely limited; and in my ignorance I had formed some very erroneous ideas of human dignity. I had learned to look upon a man of education as an awe-inspiring object of superiority, and honestly expected to find such persons wrapped in a mail of impenatrable dignity, and unbending self-importance. But during my five weeks of absence, I had met and conversed with many men of refined intelligence, but nowhere had I found my ideal of self-important arrogance in connection with education. On the other hand, I discovered that ignorance and self-conceit were invariably habitants of the same mind. It was from this latter class that I invariably met with the strongest, most uncompromising opposition. It was they who hurled the hot shot of abuse, and vociferated the cry of devil, while men of intelligence quietly investigated the phenomena. Beside these just conclusions in regard to human characteristics—which were of much educational benefit to my unenlightened mind—I learned much of the outside appearance of genteel society, and as I made a point to practice what I had gained in theory, many of my boorish habits of country verdancy were trained into acts of gentility.

In consequence of my observations and my experience of appreciated friendship, I began to feel a sort of pride for my wonderful endowments, and an outcropping aspiration for future renown began to send forth puny sprouts of germinating ambition, which heretofore had lain dormant in my mind. I suddenly saw that wealth was a powerful auxiliary of earthly happiness, and I naturally began to consider in my own mind how I could best employ my psychological gifts so as to accumulate worldly independence. I saw only one way this could be accomplished. People were fond of mystery, and my past experience had proven that if I would confine myself to the province of fortune-telling and like proceedings, that I would meet with no difficulty in amassing a comparative fortune. Consequently I resolved that I would quietly court notoriety as a revealer of the future. I imagined no opposition to this arrangement outside of the opposition of friends; but, as the sequel will prove, this conclusion was a decided mistake, and I found that I was destined to meet uncontrollable opposition to these objectionable proceedings from an entirely unexpected source. My guide—Walapaca—had once or twice warned me of peremptorial withdrawal of influence in case of an attempt at perversion of my powers, and no sooner did I commence to put my late resolution into practice than he announced an unqualified determination to put his threat in execution. At first I did not believe he had the power to rob me of my psychological abilities; but even in this I was mistaken. He said I should lose my power for one month from a certain date, and when that day arrived I found on trial that I was as impervious to magnetic influence as ever was the most positive magnetizer in existence. During this month of quietude I bitterly repented the folly that had brought about this state of affairs. My wife was forced to make all professional examinations of patients, while I, with as much calmness as I could muster, waited patiently for a renewal of my now more than ever cherished clairvoyant powers. This circumstance of loss of influence, went far to establish a belief in my mind in the phenomena of spirit communication.

Heretofore I had neither denied nor admitted any belief in the doctrine of spiritualism, and in my own mind I was not conscious of any settled conviction, either pro or con. I knew that spirit claimed to influence me, and this claim in some instances appeared to be substantiated beyond cavil or doubt. But at the same time I supposed myself capable of independent clairvoyance—supposed that, at my own pleasure, I could enter into a superior condition of psychology independent of any foreign assistance. But here was positive and convincing proof to the contrary. A person purporting to be a spirit had declared that I should lose my psychological powers for one month; he had even specified the day this loss should take place, and the reasons therefor; had told when it should return; and all through the affair there was displayed an unmistakable manifestation of intelligence. After a careful investigation, I was forced to admit two fully substantiated facts: first, that spirits could by magnetic power control me; secondly, that there was no such thing as an independent clairvoyant, and that in all cases there must be a positive operator, in some form or other. That operator, in my case, was a disembodied spirit.

CHAPTER XII.

IN WHICH I AM VICTIMIZED.—A SAMPLE OF CORRESPONDENCE.—THE TRIALS OF CLAIRVOYANCE.

MY CLAIRVOYANT powers returned on the day promised, precisely as my guide Walapaca had foretold, and I at once resumed my former mystic operations. For three years following this event my life was but a monotonous repetition of medical practice, utterly devoid of unusual incidents. During this time I had steadily advanced towards public esteem, and by a persistent adherence to my apparent mission, and an unflinching application of my marvelous powers, had won not only a professional position, but the confidence of all classes of people. Even practical M. D.'s of the Old School recognized me as a legitimate representative of Esculapius, and occasionally came to me for counsel and advice. Scientific opposition had everywhere been met by scientific and unimpeachable truths. Clairvoyance was admitted as a science, and spiritualism numbered its advocates by thousands; among whom were the greatest intellects and men of the deepest scientific education. Reason, religion, research, and philosophical investigation unwittingly contributed undeniable proof of spirit power and existence.

But my greatest strength lay in my own acts. No one could account for my marvelous powers, only by admitting me to be the medium of some foreign agency. I examined persons who were absent as well as those who were present, and medically treated hundreds of individuals whom I had never seen. Every day I was in receipt of numerous letters from all parts of the country, containing simply the name, age, and residence of the applicant. This was all I desired to insure a correct diagnosis; which, with the aid of a scribe, was written down as given by me, and forwarded back as the result of examination. This was the most astonishing part of my peculiar powers, as it effectually disproved the absurd theory of sympathetic connections, which some strongly advocated as the secret of my ability to correctly examine persons when present. And as these opposers found that their pet theory of "sympathetic relation" was insufficient as a basis of argument, they unqualifiedly asserted my written examinations to be the result of guess-work; and at once set about the task of collecting actual proof of their assertions.

One day I received a letter containing all necessary requirements and the ordinary fee, with a request for an immediate examination of the person, whom the letter reported as being dangerously ill, and in great want of immediate treatment. As usual, this case was submitted to my clairvoyant inspection. I soon discovered the individual, and found him suffering from a combination of physical derangements, and that his disease had a decided tendency toward consumption. I also saw that he could be considerably helped - perhaps nearly cured—by one prescription, hence I proceeded to specify the medicine. My scribe, who had written down the examination, sent that along with the prescription to the individual who, according to the letter, had written for his suffering friend.

Let the reader judge of my surprise and indignation upon receiving a letter stating that Mr. Burnham (the person I had examined), was a man in the enjoyment of more than ordinary good health; that there was no signs of consumption or any other disease about him; that as far as he knew he was perfectly well, and that they had only written to me to prove just what they had proven, namely: that so far as my written examinations were concerned I was purely a "cheat."

The result of this examination was heralded all over the country, and so far as appearances were concerned, the affair was wholly against clairvoyance. But the joy of my opposers was of short duration. There suddenly sprung up a new phase to the affair, which in some respects was quite startling, even to the parties concerned. In the first place, Mr. Burnham, who reported himself as being "perfectly well," was within a week from the date of my examination attacked with an unexpected combination of diseases, which at last terminated in consumption; and in less than six months he found it necessary to apply the very prescription I had sent him. Secondly, it was soon ascertained by some of my friends, that there resided in the same town another individual by the name of Burnham, who at the time of the examination was suffering with the complaints I had described. In all probability, this person was the one whom I first examined, for on examination I found his condition unchanged. This supposition is perfectly reasonable. I had been furnished with the name, age, and residence of an individual who was said to be suffering from a disease, and taking it for granted that this statement was true, my guide sought for a person answering to the name, age, and other description, without stopping to examine the real motives of the writer, or even supposing there could be a mistake. The person sought was found; his name was Burnham; the age given in the letter was the probable age of this person; he was a resident of the town in which it was said this Mr. Burnham resided; and, moreover, this person was "dangerously ill, and in great want of immediate treatment."

Everything corresponded to directions in letter, and my guide sought for a person answering to the description given the same as any person would who was following the directions of a third party, in a similar instance; finding the facts to be true, to the writer's direction, he had no reasons for enquiring into his motives, therefore naturally fell into error. Had he found the other Burnham first, the case would have been different, and he would have considered the letter in part a tissue of falsehood, and this would have led to an investigation of the author's motive for writing.

This case in the end proved to be more beneficial to me than injurious, inasmuch as it furnished a chance for self-vindication, and led to a more extended knowledge of the principles of clairvoyance, which by many was looked upon as being a power nearly akin to the infinite, and therefore incapable of error.

The reader is supposed to know by this time the leading traits of my mental organization. Perhaps the strongest element was an almost irresistible impulse to respond to demands made upon my time by suffering humanity. On receiving a letter from a stranger appealing for relief from some trial or disease, I would be immediately disposed to return a humane and beneficial answer—oftimes in direct violation of the law of self-justice and self-preservation. This natural proclivity exposed me to much imposition and annoyance. Yet I have no desire that I should by nature be less disposed to universal good-will, for in this principle I have found the germ of all my earthly happiness, and I would rather be the victim of an occasional imposition, and suffer the annoyance therefrom than to feel that I was by nature selfish.

My fame as a clairvoyant, and the great scarcity at that time of similarly endowed persons, brought me scores upon scores of letters from all classes of persons. The greater portion were from persons who were half sick or half dead with various diseases. These desired examination and medical treatment, and were always promptly attended to. But besides these, I was in daily receipt of letters containing every conceivable shade of scientific, historical, domestic, and philosophical inquiry—never imparting a particle of information, but asking innumerable questions about all sorts of out-of-the-way and never-before-thought-of subjects. If the task of spelling and reading these epistles was arduous, as it was, how shall I describe the toiling that was necessary to answer them? From one correspondent's letter I extract the following:

MICHIGAN, 1860.

"MY DEAR SIR:—I feel forced to seek some more information from you, for I am in a great dilemma. It appears that the spirits are determined not to leave me. Why they should torment me thus is more than I can understand. I want to know what I can do to get rid of them. I am confident that you have the power to exorcise them; and now if you will enable me to become once more free from their influence, I will pay you for your trouble. Please answer me soon. Yours, &c."

I had received a former letter from this individual, in which he had stated that he believed himself susceptible to spirit influence, and he desired me to send him a formula of the *modus operandi* necessary to his development. This I had done. He was now tired of the influence, and desired to be rid of his altogether too attentive spirit friends. My reply was that I had no power to exorcise spirits—that all my time was occupied in examining the sick—that the spirits would not hurt him—and that if he really desired to be free, he could be by simply asserting a man-like strength of purpose. Ten days later the post brought me another letter from the same person, in which he said:

"All hope is lost. I am a ruined man—a victim of infernal witchcraft! Had I not listened to your counsel, I should have to-day been free from the machinations of the devil, and there would have been a hope of salvation; but by your infernal powers I am debarred from the Church, and made the subject of the devil."

And thus did the half-crazed man rail against me. Evidently he was the victim of priestly influence, and had been made to believe that these spirit manifestations were the workings of evil spirits, who were bent upon his destruction. To these rantings I made no reply, for I saw that the man was too ignorant to comprehend an explanation. Next I would read over a package of fifty letters containing reasonable inquiries, and then there would come a request of this kind:

DETROIT, MICH.

"RESPECTED SIR:—I have been informed that you can tell the past and future of all persons' lives, and I have determined to consult you, and see if you can tell the past events, and also the things pertaining to the future in my life. I want to know if the contents of the letter I have just received are true, or is it deception; and if true, can you tell me where it came from? Is my husband true to me? Will he out-live me? Will my future life be more happy than my past has been? Now, for God's sake, do not deceive me, but tell me all about myself, and I will believe you to be the most wonderful man living.

With great respect, &c."

My only reply to this was that I did not undertake to reveal the future, and that, in mv estimation, all pretended fortune-tellers were arrant knaves.

Almost every day I was in receipt of letters containing questions like the following:

"If I make an investment in the C——— stock company, will I receive pecuniary profit?" "Can you tell me where I can negotiate a loan on the securities in my possession?" "Will my present matrimonial prospects be a success?" "Can you at any time, and on short notice, determine the state of the markets?" And so on to an inconceivable extent.

To have answered one-half of the questions asked would have required almost infinite knowledge; yet the writers honestly supposed me equal to the task. Let the reader bear in remembrance, while glancing over these few "wants" from the world that I have been the daily recipient of similar demands for twelve years, and you can then form some idea of the amount accumulated, and the consequent troubles and trials to which I have been exposed. One more illustration from this heterogeneous mass of correspondence will suffice:

DR. D. B. KELLOGG, *Sir:*—Pardon a stranger's writing to you upon a personal subject. But as I have heard of your wonderful power, I thought perhaps you might be able to help me out of a great trouble. I am a hunted criminal. If I am captured

I shall be incarcerated for life. I have for six months eluded pursuit; but I am now fearful of being taken, for I have reason to believe the officers of the law have discovered my whereabouts, and what I want you to do is to tell me where I shall go to be safe. I am confident you can do this if you will; so I hope you will not let conscientious scruples debar you from aiding a persecuted fellow being, but tell me at once where I shall flee."

This letter was never answered, and it is only one of several of like description. Thus, dear reader, I lived, a subject of continual misrepresentation—a being of finite powers, supposed, even by men of intelligence, to be endowed with supernatural abilities.

How long will the science of spiritualism remain a mystery to the world?

CHAPTER XIII.

A CHANGE OF RESIDENCE AND A CHANGE OF SUBJECT.

IN THE spring of 1865 I executed a secretly premeditated idea of change of residence. My reasons for this remove was owing to my rapid increase in business and the inconvenience of my present locality. I was every day sending medicines to all parts of the country by express, and as it was six miles to the nearest express office, the task was neither pleasant nor profitable. Besides this, my fame for removing cancers was causing a rapid increase of practice in this direction, it became absolutely necessary for me to enlarge my infirmary conveniences. But where to go was the question. I had numerous warm friends who desired me to open an office in the thriving city of Ypsilanti. But somehow my own inclinations prompted me to take up my abode in Ann Arbor. This place I knew to be the great northwestern emporium of medical knowledge; I farther knew that two or three clairvoyant physicians had undertaken to locate there but had ingloriously failed. But, notwithstanding these facts, I resolved to take up my residence there, and trust myself to the tender mercies of an intelligent community.

My reception to the new home was not only pleasant but entirely unexpected, and I looked upon it as a brilliant foreshadowing of the future. Rumors of my coming had gone before me, and on my arrival I found quite a respectful gathering of people, who were all anxious to get a glimpse of the "mysterious doctor," and have an examination of their case. Anxious to please I at once threw aside my coat, entered the office which had been prepared for me, and began my mystic labors. Every person, even those who were skeptical in belief, were satisfied with my ability, consequently my reputation as a physician was at once established. I here, as usual, courted investigation, and publicly announced that I desired to be tested by the scientific world. This announcement brought before me men of professional education, scientific doctors, and even members of the Faculty. But after a few sittings they quietly withdrew apparently satisfied that I was, as far as possible, master of my profession, and the medium of a medical knowledge of no mean pretentions; and they no doubt saw that the appellation of "quack" would hardly be applicable in my case on account of the great number of favorable testimonials in my possession, and my mysterious capability to render correct diagnosis of disease and analytical knowledge of medical properties.

And here I have since remained, the daily recipient of many kind favors. But what gives me the greatest amount of unalloyed satisfaction is the knowledge that my ardous labors have been appreciated by a just community. When worn out with continuous toil, I find a balm to my care worn spirit in listening to the voluntary outpouring of a heart-felt gratitude, coming from some former suffering fellow being who has, through my agency, been restored to health and the happiness of life.

In this mission I feel I have found the acme of my soul's aspiration. In my present capacity all the better promptings of my nature are brought in play. Hence, I have, for several years, ceased to make any endeavor for any further psychological advancement. My operations at present are carried on by means of dependent clairvoyance; and to arrive at this peculiar psychological state I have been forced to pass through all the lower order of spiritual influences, as the reader who has read the previous pages, must have discovered. It will be seen that my present position is but the result of psychological developments. My knowledge of the human organism and of medicine has all been derived by clairvoyant powers. I have made one or two attempts to gain information from books, but have, on such trial, failed to receive satisfaction. Still I do not condemn books as a means of education, for I am well aware that there are but very few who are like myself.

In the foregoing pages I have hastily noted the major points in my psychological life; of my personal career as a man, as a member of society, I have studiously avoided speaking, as I have considered that part uninteresting to the general reader. The question most often asked is, how I became what I am, professionally? This query I have endeavored to illustrate. What my individual trials and troubles have been no one can have any desire to know.

But my task is not yet done, there is something yet remaining. I have told how I became a physician, how I became a clairvoyant. But the reason why I am so remains to be told, as well as the philosophy of these various mysterious psychological phases through which I have passed. The query arises, what is spiritualism? what is magnetism? and what is clairvoyance? and what is necessary to development? For me to state that I am a clairvoyant does not illustrate the phenomena, or that I am the medium of spirits does not prove spiritualism. My life proves there is a mystery some where, but does not make that mystery plain. In view of this I have concluded to give a concise explanation of the mysteries involved in my career.

CHAPTER XIV.

THE PHILOSOPHY OF MAGNETISM, AND ITS RELATION TO ORDINARY SLEEP, AND THE SCIENCE OF SPIRITUALISM.

IN ORDER to arrive at an intelligent understanding of clairvoyance, or even spirit manifestations, it becomes absolutely necessary that the principles of mesmerism should be understood, for mesmerism is the foundation of every phase of psychological phenomena. In Chapter IV I have given an acconnt of my first mesmeric experience, and I now propose to give a condensed explanation of the natural principles involved in the phenomena.

Webster defines the term mesmerism "to be the art of communicating a *species* of sleep to the body, while the mind remains active." The pertinent question which here naturally arises is " what species of sleep is it that is by the power of mesmerism communicated ? " I take the ground that there is no difference between sleep induced by mesmerism and natural slumber, so far as principles are concerned. This ground, I shall, in this chapter, aim to illustrate by a comparison of the two phenomena. In order to do this it becomes necessary for me to consider the philosophy of ordinary sleep; and to do this I must take into consideration the nervous organization of the human body, and from thence deduce inferences in regard to the elementary principles of ordinary slumber. The nervous system of the human organism is divided into two grand parts: being the brain and spinal cord, and these combined are known as the *cerebro-spinal centres.* From this axis or centre, there are numerous nerves which run to all parts of the system. A portion of these nerves start from the base of the brain and terminate in the eye, the ear, the tongue, the lips, etc. This set of nerves are the first developed in the infantile organism. Another and larger portion of nerves spring from the spinal cord, and are distributed over the body and lower extremities. By means of a portion of these nerves the brain is susceptible of sensation or feeling, while the others produce motion. These two set of nerves are widely distributed over the entire body, and as I have inferred, have distinct duties to perform. Those which spring from the spinal cord have two roots, one uniting with the *back;* the other with the *front* part of the cord. If we could cut the back root we would find that the part where the nerve terminates would loose the sense of feeling but retain the power of motion. By cutting the front root, we would destroy the power of motion, while the sense of feeling would be retained; and by severing both, we would find that the sense of feeling and power of motion would be lost.

These facts prove, first: nervous duality, and distinction of nervous functions. Secondly: that it is only by means of the sensient portions of these nerves that the mind can become cognizant of external objects; or in other words, all recognized impressions and sensations must be borne by the nerves to the brain. These two sets of nerves operate comparatively like the Telegraphic Fire Alarms of some of our great Cities. The brain, being the intelligent center, may be compared to the central office, and the nerves of sensation which carry to the brain with lightning-like speed intelligence of what is going on out-side, are like the wires which run from the central office to the several station boxes. The quick sensation of injury or danger to the body which is borne along these nerves to the brain, is like sending to the central office from a station box the intelligence of fire in one of the districts. The rapid transmission of orders from the mind to the muscle, is like flashing the alarm over the wires to all parts of the city. The sensorium of the brain is like the voltaic battery at the central office; while the ideal powers of mind, may be compared to the operator. When no intelligence is being received from the station boxes, or imported from the operator, the battery is in a state of complete inactivity; and the same is true in respect to the sensorium of the brain; which may be considered as always asleep—or in a state of inactivity—unless aroused by external causes; or by internal demands from the ideal.

Evidently sensation from the external world can reach the brain only by coming in contact with the outward terminus of the sentient nerves; while individual motives and power of muscular activity have their origin in the higher faculties of the mind. Which oft-times by the power of memory, appears to prompt muscular motion in the same manner that the fire alarm telegraph operator is moved to action; by his remembrance of what is necessary for him to do in the case of an alarm of fire. Taking this view of the subject, and admitting it to be a fact in principle, we readily see that the sensorium is the medium of two positive extremes; and, that while the nerves of sense retain their normal powers, that the sensorium cannot resist impressional encroachment. Hence, in order that the brain—ideal and sensorial—may become irrecognizant of surroundings, it is plain that there must be a pervertion or suspension of nervous power to transmit sensation. In sleep, we have a practical manifestation of this phenomena, viz.: suspension of nervous power to transmit sensation. Sleep, therefore, is dormancy of nervous sense, instead of dormancy of the sensorium and ideal powers; for both of these latter powers may be in a state of activity, while a person is in a condition of profound sensient slumber—a fact illustrated by somnambulists and somniloquists.

There is no gradation limits in the phenomena of ordinary sleep. When a person slumbers they are devoid of every faculty of sense, they can neither hear, see, smell, taste, or feel; do not recognize pain, and have no knowledge of personal movements; in short, are dead to all external surroundings, and to everything but the ideal powers of their own mind; and this result is simply because the nervous fluid is in a state of lethargy, superinduced by one or the other of the following causes of sleep, namely: muscular or sensorial fatigue; narcotic influence; compression of brain; or induction of electro-magnetism sufficient to cause sensuous inactivity: or more properly, magnetic slumber, and this is what is termed mesmerism.

Sleep resulting from muscular and nervous fatigue, is the ordinary phenomena of healthy slumber, and to arrive at this condition is an every day experience. By exercise, the nervous system suffers such a change that it becomes reduced to a condition requiring inactivity, and recuperative rest; or in other words, continuous action, so exhausts the nervous system that it naturally bec: mes indisposed to nervous action. It is while in this condition that a sensation of sleepiness is felt. Stronger or more interesting external impression, or stronger ideal, or intellectual tendencies are necessary to keep one awake after great nervous fatigue than before. While in this condition, if one retires from a noise to a soft couch he has only to close his eyes, so as to obstruct the power of vision, and discontinues to make demand upon the nerves of sense by bringing the higher faculties of the mind to a state of tranquility, to cause these nerves of sense to naturally relapse into a complete state of inactivity. We may therefore consider nervous exhaustion as the primary, predisposing cause of sleep; and the avoiding of external impression as the more immediate cause; and that ordinary slumber is simply inertia of sense. While a person is in a condition of ordinary or even magnetic sleep, I do not believe that the concient action of the nerves of sense or sensorium of the brain are stopped by an accumulation of blood within the brain; for I can see no possible need of any such supposition. But in a case of sleep produced by narcotics, there is some reason to suppose that the vessels of the brain become distended with blood, and thereby obstruct the action of the concient nerves; and this is the probable result in cases of compression, which sometimes results in morbid sleep. When there can be no consient action of the brain aroused, there can be no nervous sensation excited; for the co-existence of a concient action of the organic and cerebral extremities of a nerve is as essential to a sensation, as two tongs put together are to a pair of tongs.

It is erroneous to suppose that the ideal powers of mind, (meaning by this term the faculties of thought, memory, and the motive powers of action,) are necessarily reduced to a condition of slumber during nervous inactivity of sense or sleep. Dreams are the result of ideal wakefulness and activity: and the walking and talking phenomena characteristic of somnambulists and somniloquists prove, that a person may be bereft of the powers of nervous sensation or feeling, and still retain intellectual or ideal wakefulness and active motive powers; thus proving that sleep is merely suspension of inductive nervous sensation, or dormancy of that portion of organic nerves which are employed in conveying sense from external objects to the sensorium of the brain.

What the peculiar elementary proportion of the nervous organization are, is an unsettled subject of investigation. Sir Benjamin Brodie, says: "that the nervous force is probably some modification of that force which produces the phenomena of electricity and magnetism." The probable idea designed to be conveyed, is, that the nervous fluid or force, is both electrical and magnetic; hence, positive and negative. We have seen that there are two sets of nerves peculiar to the human organism, and that one of these sets are absorbents or magnetic courses, leading from the external world to the brain. This set is defined as the nerves of sense; and these are evidently (owing to their absorbent powers) susceptible to magnetic induction to an extent sufficient to cause inactivity, therefore may be considered as the negative power; while the other set leading from the brain, directly and indirectly, by means of the spinal cord, and which we have seen—are the medial cause of motion, may be considered the positive individual power. We may reasonably suppose that this latter set of nerves are charged with an electrode force or agent generated in the brain and spinal cord by the metal bearing fluid and electro generating powers of the blood, by a process comparatively like the action of the acid solutions on the metalic plates in the cells of an ordinary voltaic battery. This theory of electric generating power of the brain is pretty well substantiated by well known physiological facts. One-fifth of the blood in the human organism goes into the sensorium of the brain. Hamatin, one of the constituents of the blood, contains about eight per-cent of iron; while other portions contain, in smaller quantities, other metals. Hence, taking into consideration the quantity of blood sent to the brain, in connection with the fact that its metalic constituents are favorable to electric generation, it appears reasonable to infer that the cerebral battery (I use this term in default of a more accurate one) is charged by the electric chemical action of these metalic properties of the blood. If this theory of electric generation be true, the brain may be considered as an electric reservoir, from which originate the primary powers of muscular action. From this it will be seen that the nerves of motion may act independent of the nerves of sense. In fact, it is only by making this division of the nervous powers that we can explain the phenomena of sleep or stupefaction of the powers of sense, in connection with ideal wakefulness and muscular motion displayed by somnambulists and somniloquists. No one will deny but what these two phenomenas do coexist. Dreams, are simply a phrase of somnambulism, and there is hardly a person but what is subject to dreams.

There are many logical proofs of this theory of distinct nervous power; but I imagine that sufficient has been offered to illustrate my position in regard to duality of nervous powers and the phenomena of sleep.

I hold that sleep, both ordinary and mesmeric, is simply cessation of the powers of sense, and that to arrive at either of these conditions it is not absolutely necessary that the electric powers of the brain should become dormant; or, in other words, I contend that while a person is in a condition of absolute stupefaction of the organic nerves of sense, he may retain the ideal and motive powers of mind in a condition of activity. Hence the peculiar species of sleep communicated by the art of mesmerism is the same as is manifested in ordinary sleep, namely: dormancy of the five organic faculties of sense. Let the reader bear in mind that I am here considering the art of mesmerism in its lowest degree, as a sleep producing and organic controlling power, without any regard to its higher or psychological influence over the mental powers. I have said that ordinary sleep was the legitimate effect of nervous fatigue or exhaustion, and that slumber produced by narcotics or compression of the brain, is the result of forced stupefaction of the cerebral extremity of the nerves of sense; and mesmeric slumber was caused by an induction of an electric current sufficient to overcome the positive force of the nerves of sensation. Each of these phases of sleep are subject to the same law, and all are in fact one in principle, being the result of a disturbance of the natural equilibrium existing between the two extremities of the nerves of sense.

To produce the magnetic coma, it is necessary the natural force of sense should be overcome by the introduction of a more positive magnetic power, or, in other words, a positive and negative power must be brought in conjunction. This positive power is that magnetic current which imperceptibly flows from one body to another, as a sensational medium. Ordinary sensation is a simple phase of magnetism; all objects which attract the mind are positive to the mind, to the full extent of the attraction ; and those which repel are to the same extent negative. This fact is demonstrated by our sympathies and antipathies, our likes and dislikes, our attractions and repulsions. Nervous sensation, being thus closely allied to vital magnetism. we find that, in order to induce magnetic sleep, there must be certain necessary qualifications. First, there must be an absolute negative and positive power; secondly, the equilibrium existing between the two extremities (cerebral and organic) of the nervous organism of the negative power or subject, must be disturbed by the positive power, or operator. These principles are absolute, being, as they are, the fundamental basis of the law of attraction and organic connection, or combined action of separate organism. When these absolute conditions exist, the phenomena of magnetic sleep may be produced by adhering to simple rules of operation. The subject, who of course must be the negative, has only to sit in an easy position and concentrate his or her gaze steadily and calmly upon some convenient object, designated by the operator. Tranquility of mind, calm concentration of gaze, and willingness to enter the magnetic sleep, is all that is required of the subject.

While the subject is in this required condition, the operator—who must be the positive power—must regard him or her visually and mentally with a fixed, determined, and definite purpose, to overcome nervous activity. After doing this for about two minutes, the operator should breathe gently on the face and head of the subject, and this should be continued until the subject manifests optical fatigue. Then let the operator raise his hands gently above the subject's head, and bring them down softly, brushing the sides of the head; place them upon the shoulders, and let them rest there for one minute; then continue the downward motion, with a gentle sweep, to the tips of the fingers; raise them with a spiral movement, and return them, with the palms outward, to the head as before. This manipulating process should be continued for twenty or thirty minutes. Where the subject is extremely nervous or sensitive, it is necessary for the operator to take his position several feet from them. There is no necessity for muscular effort on the part of the magnetizer. His movements should not be rapid, but easy, graceful, and attractive. These simple processes are all that is necessary to produce the phenomena of mesmerism; providing, the before mentioned absolute requirement exist, namely: positive and negative powers.

There are various other formulas besides this in vogue among magnetic operators, but all additions are simply gotten up for mystic effect.

Two questions naturally arise: First, what are the sensations experienced by the subject? and secondly, what changes are there wrought in the organism of the subject by this manipulatory process, providing there should be a magnetic effect? In Chapter III, I have given a partial account of my own experience and sensations while under magnetic influence. The first sensation is generally experienced in the visual nerves of the eye. This sensation is very much like that experienced by a person who has looked at the noonday sun until his eyesight has become dimmed or blurred; next, if the eyes are closed, the lids of the eyes will assume a feeling of extreme heaviness, which will increase in power until they utterly lose the sense of feeling, and if the operator continues his manipulations according to the above formula, the arms and hands will be subject to an increasing volume of paralyzing numbness and cold, until sensation utterly fails. When the subject is in complete magnetic condition he is bereft of every faculty of sense.

Many suppose that when a person is magnetized they experience a prickly sensation, peculiar to that felt in case of stagnation of the blood. This idea, I think, is entirely erroneous—at least my own extensive experience proves it so to be. I never experienced any physical sensation different from the sensations of ordinary sleep. I make this assertion, well knowing that many others have given contrary testimony—have testified that they have experienced most horrid physical sensations during magnetic slumber—all of which I believe to be purely imaginary, or willful deception on their part. That the introduction of an electro-magnetic current produces contraction of the muscles—which to the casual observer might appear to cause suffering to the subject—I readily admit; but that the subject experiences any such sense of suffering, I deny; for contraction of the muscles by magnetic power cannot be produced until the nerves of sense are in a state of stupefaction.

In considering the changes wrought in the organism of a person under magnetic effect, it becomes necessary to enquire into the properties and power of electro-magnetism. The extreme change, I have already said, was stupefaction of sense; but how sense is stupefied, becomes the dominant query.

It is universally admitted that all bodies, both animate and inanimate, contain a subtle fluid called natural electricity, which is composed of two contrary fluids, termed positive and negative electricity. That these fluids consist of an infinite number of small particles, which possess attractive and repulsive powers, is also admitted. While bodies are at rest these fluids are counterbalanced, or in other words, then the attractive power of one of the fluids is conquered by the repulsive power of the other. Hence, to cause magnetism, there must be a decomposition of one of these electric powers. This decomposition is brought about by a disturbance in the equilibrium naturally existing between the positive and negative powers. The disturbance which takes place in the organism of the subject is caused by an induced current of active electricity, emanating from the operator, which has power to repel the sensational medium of the nerves, from the external to the internal surface, thereby making the operator and subject, so far as the positive and negative forces are concerned, as one body. Or, in other words, the magnetizer, who is the positive force, by his superior active electric power forces a portion of that principle, which in the normal state of the subject formed the medium of sensation, from the organic terminus of the nerve into the cerebro-spinal centres and the centres pertaining to the anterior portion of the brain; and, in consequence of the departure of the elements of sensation from the nervous channels of the body, the latter is reduced to a senseless, death-like slumber. Hence, magnetic slumber is produced by electrically increasing the positive principle of natural electricity contained in a body to an extent sufficient to destroy the equilibrium existing between the attractive and repulsive powers. All positives control their negatives the moment equalization, or equilibrium is destroyed.

To deny mesmerism, or deny that magnetic coma can be produced, is synonomous to a denial of animal electric power, and the law of attraction and repulsion. Animal electric power is undeniable. The electric manifestations of the torpedo, or electric ray, and gymnotus, or electric eel, fully proves that animal life is subject to continuous disturbance in the equilibrium of the molecules, or electric particles of the body; and that every disturbance is accompanied by a liberation of active electricity; and the phenomena of receiving shocks from these animals proves that the sensoient nerves are natural absorbents of foreign electro currents. There are many, who, while they admit self-evident animal electric power, utterly deny the phenomena of animal magnetism; but upon what they base their admission of the one and denial of the other is incomprehensible, seeing that both phenomena are but different phases of the same cause. Magnetism is dependent upon electricity as a primary principle, or first cause; and electricity is dependent upon magnetism for means of manifestation of power. The shocks of the gymnotus in some instances cause numbness of of sense, in other instances it has been known to have no effect. Flagg gives an account of a lady of his acquaintance who could handle this fish at will. This person could not have been magnetized at all, and if all were like her impervious to electricity, electric power must have remained a matter of speculation; for we only know its powers by its effect. Electricity produced by artificial means will, when applied in a continuous current, produce inactivity of sense upon a person who is in a proper magnetic condition, and this fact proves that certain conditions are necessary to electric manifestations, regardless of source or fundamental power. Hence, when a subject is in a proper condition he may be controlled by electric power emanating from a positive operator.

To say that the human organism cannot emit a current of electricity, is simply absurd; for if they can receive they can impart. We might as well contend that a cloud charged with electricity does not emit a bolt of lightning, as to say that man has no power to discharge a current of electricity; for if there is an electric current in the human organism there must be a continuous discharge, in exact proportion to accumulation, in order to keep up equilibrium. When this equilibrium is destroyed, paralysis of the nervous centres must nesessarily follow, and this paralysis is simply magnetic coma. Lightning produces paralysis by a powerful induction of concentrated electricity. A ray of sunlight direct upon the eye causes paralysis of the nerves of the eye, by continuous induction of the same power. In either case the result is the same, and is simply sensuous inactivity, or lethargy of the senscient nerves.

There is a great amount of personal testimony substantiative of the phenomena of magnetism. Even in the days of Mesmer, those who opposed it as a science admitted its wonderful effects, as may be seen by a perusal of the report made by the medical faculty of Paris, in 1784. Notwithstanding this report was unfavorable to the pretentions of Mesmer, it failed to uproot the outward manifestations of the phenomena. Hence, in 1826 another commission was formed to furnish another report. These commissioners were compelled to be more careful in their investigations, for the public—owing to their increase in knowledge of the phenomena—stood ready to take the right of judgment into their own possession. These jurors rendered a more favorable verdict than did their predecessors. The following is an abstract of their conclusions. After admitting "that sleep may be produced under circumstances in which the subjects have not been able to perceive, and have been ignorant of the agency employed to occasion the slumber," they unqualifiedly assert that "the real effects produced by magnetism are very varied. It agitates some, calms others; it usually accelerates the respiration and circulation; causes convulsive motions similar to electric shocks, a lassitude, and torpor more or less profound; somnolence, and in a limited number of cases what was by the operator denominated somnambulism." They admitted that often "remarkable changes" took place in the perceptions and faculties of certain individuals in whom somnambulism was produced by magnetic passes. They considered it certain that the somnambulic state did exist, and were equally certain that it gave rise to the development of new faculties, which then, as now, was designated by the term, "Clairvoyance, intuition, and internal perception."

These conclusions were published by a professionally prejudiced commission; yet apparent facts forced them to admit all the power that has ever been claimed for the phenomena of mesmerism, namely: human magnetism, somnambulism, and clairvoyance. Since this famous report was published to the world, there has been a continuous accumulation of testimony favorable to the phenomena. There is hardly a person but what has witnessed its manifestations, and thousands have personally experienced mesmeric influence. And yet, with all the mass of evidence which is extant—highly confirmatory of the principles of magnetism—there is a class of supercilious pedagogues, and disciples of electric science, who attribute all the phases of magnetic phenomena to imposture or imagination. This class of pompous investigators must find a certain degree of gall in the admission of the profound thinker, LA PLACE, who says, in speaking of magnetism, that "We are so far from being acquainted with all the agents of nature, that it would be quite unphilosophical to deny the existence of the phenomena, merely because they are inexplicable in the present state of our knowledge." The celebrated Cuvier contradicts the idea that mesmerism is the result of imagination. He says: "The effect on persons ignorant of the cause, and upon persons whom the operation itself has deprived of consciousness, and those effects which animals present, do not permit us to doubt that the proximity of two animal bodies, in certain electrical conditions, combined with certain movements, have a real effect, independent of all participations of fancy.

Spiritualists hold that mesmerism is the medium or vehicle of the very highest codes of morality and divine intelligence; and for this reason, men of clerical pretentions deny the existence of magnetic agency or electric intercourse, between mind and body. These men first clamor for recognizance of their ideas of ancient inspiration and modern assistance of the spirit, and at the same time deny the only means by which the phenomena of inspiration could be accomplished. They admit the power, but deny the means, and at the same time clamor for the result. Their arguments are so inconsistently absurd that it would be folly to notice them were it not for their seeming popularity.

No science has struggled through more opposition than has this one of magnetism. It has, in the hands of arrant charlatans, been made the basis of mystic operations; has suffered gross abuse from impostors and superficial observers; has been condemned by men of learning, and extravagantly upheld by others of equal intelligence. Yet, in spite of all, it has obtained a modest position among the sciences, which day by day is increasing in brilliancy through the instrumentality of spirit intercourse. For its moral utility, I have only to refer you to the millions of our own countrymen who have been led from physical darkness into spiritual light by its developments, and to the thousands who are daily testifying to its physical utility, in all parts of the world.

CHAPTER XV.

SOMNAMBULISM AND CLAIRVOYANCE EXPLAINED.

I HAVE said in the preceding chapter that while a subject was under magnetic control, much of that principle which in the normal state forms the medium of sensation, goes into the cerebro-spinal centers, and other centers which pertain to the anterior, or front part of the brain, producing the external phenomena of magnetic coma. But this does not comprehend the entire sesult; for in proportion as the body is deadened the mind is enlivened, for the natural elements of the mind are then all absorbed in the brain, except enough to maintain the moderate performance of the organic functions. When the mind is enlivened through the means of sensient stupefaction, by magnetic induction, somnambulism is the result.

Somnambulism may be produced naturally, or it may be superinduced by manipulations; but in either case the somnambulist must be devoid of the powers of sense. It matters not how this state is obtained, for the result—or manifestations—are invariably the same in character, but frequently different in degree.

Some persons while in this condition possess but little more than ordinary perception and power of accomplishment, while others manifest much more than their usual clearness of intellect, and energy of muscles. In nearly all cases, the same individual when awake, and when somnambulic, appears like two entirely different characters. How these entirely different conditions can be exhibited in one individual, becomes an interesting question. Eminent experimental philosophers have elucidated, to a certain extent, the idea that the entire organism of Nature is pervaded with a spiritual or vitalizing principle, which is diffused throughout all the wide realms of creation. This vitalizing principle is like the medium of sensation, which permeates the human body, and is the means of communication between all bodies in nature. It is the vehicle of thought, of sense, of sympathy—in short, it is the connecting link between mind and matter, and between object and object. It is the vitalizing medium that gives to the mind or spirit power to manifest intelligence. It is the grand vehicle of universal influence; and is the great harmonizer of the universe. For, in pervading and traversing bodies, it modifies them and is equally modified by them in turn, and where it circulates from one body to another with the same force or power, these two bodies are maintained in harmonious relations, one towards the other. It is through the instrumentality of this fluid that our nerves receive sensations from surrounding objects or bodies. Being the medium of sympathy, it is the underlying principle of social order, and the operative means of intelligence. The mind slopes our actions in accordance with the idea conveyed by this all pervading fluid.

Man is a two-fold being; besides the external organs of sense—the nerves—he is endowed with corresponding internal organs of sensibility. The nerves are the magnetic plexus or wires, which connect the interior being with the objective world; they are a bridge upon which the exact image of external objects and influences travel into the sensorium; and by their means alone the spirit holds converse with the outer world. It is the mind alone that sees, hears, feels, and reflects; all else, so far as innate powers are concerned, is blind, deaf, dead; for the body is but the vestment of the mind—the clothing of the spirit—with sense adapted to the present mode of existence. Hence, the vitalizing principle—the medium of sensation—which permeates the nervous system, is but a protracted extension of mind. As the branches which diverge from the bowl of the tree are a part of the tree, so is the nervous system which springs from the brain a part of the brain. The vitalizing principle in the smallest twig is the same in kind as that which permeates the boll; so the vitalizing principle of the nerves is synonomous to the same element in the sensorium. The frosts of winter send a large portion of the vitalizing principle contained in the twig back into the boll or roots, the reservoir from whence it sprang; so the equilibrium-destroying powers of magnetism send the vitalizing principle of the nervous system, which is the medium of sensation, back into its fountain or reservoir, which is the sensorium of the brain.

When this vital principle which before pervaded the external organism is by magnetic power transferred to the interior department of the brain, the mind, in some instances, appears to be impressed with delicate and sublime ideas; and often an individual is made to appear, in deportment and expression, as another person. At times, individuals of ordinary natural abilities have been known to give expression to profound and refined intelligence while in a condition of natural somnambulism. The reasoning powers of others appear to be intensified, and unusually vigorous and successful. Ambercrombie adduces a remarkable example of intensified powers of reason, while in a somnambulic condition, in the case of a distinguished lawyer of the last century, which is as follows: "This eminent person had been consulted respecting a case of great importance and much difficulty, and he had been studying it with intense anxiety and attention. After several days had been occupied in this manner, he was observed by his wife to rise from his bed in the night, and go to a writing desk which stood in the bed-room. He then sat down and wrote a long paper, which he carefully put by in the desk and returned to bed. The following morning he told his wife that he had had a most interesting dream; that he had dreamed of delivering a clear and luminous opinion respecting a case which had exceedingly perplexed him, and he would give anything to recover the train of thought which had passed before him in his sleep. She then directed him to the writing desk, where he found the opinion, clearly and fully written out. It was afterward found to be perfectly correct."

In this instance, the reasoning powers of the sleeper were perceptibly intensified ; and this phenomena was, in all probability, in consequence of inactivity of sense. External objects could not distract or pervert the mind, hence there was nothing to prohibit concentration of thought.

Man's visible physical organization, being, as it is, the cradle of the spirit, is perfectly adapted to the objects and convolving circumstances of the external world. The higher aspirations of the rapt soul or mind is often chained down by the sensuous conditions of life. But sometimes, when these sensuous conditions are laid aside in sleep, the unchained mind soars into brighter, purer, loftier spheres, and the ordinary man appears to be gifted with new powers of thought. The poet who, with energies unfettered by sense, depicts the loveliness of our spiritual nature, is like the somnambulist, whose impressions are often very distinct and delightful, because the attention and sensibilities of the mind are no longer perverted or distracted by the intrusion of impressions from the outer world, which is common in the ordinary or working state.

Somnambulism may be philosophically considered

as the incipient manifestations of mind, unaided by the organic organs of sense; or, in other words, it is an independent demonstration of the soul, a manifestation of innate ideas, which are uncontrolled by counter-acting perception. Ideas have their origin in the mind, while perceptions are the offspring of sense. Somnambulism is not clairvoyance. Clairvoyance means clear vision. The clairvoyant sees objects, and can analyze and describe them; but the somnambulist sees nothing, nor does he comprehend anything outside of his own mind. Every idea to which they give utterance comes from their garnered store of knowledge, and though they may promulgate ideas more exalted than they are wont to when in an ordinary state, still these ideas can have no other origin than in their individual mind, unless there is magnetic connection between the somnambule and some foreign intelligence of sufficient power to cause the Hypnotic phenomena, of which I shall speak hereafter.

The state of somnambulism is a condition totally different from that of ordinary life. The animal sensibilities undergo an essential change, and the ordinary activity of the corporeal faculties are for a time suspended. But the ideal mind—the immaterial principle—the very soul itself—displays its unfettered energies independent of the material organs. Thoughts which have been garnered into the mind by study, but which have been held there by the controlling powers of sense, find means of utterance while the senses sleep.

The well-authenticated phenomena of magnetic somnambulism is, in this day of progressive science, a weapon of mighty power in the field of human scepticism. As electricity explains the thunder, as astronomy explains the appearance of comets and the causes of eclipses, so human magnetism explains the mystic phenomena formerly attributed to magic and witchcraft, which in past days of ignorance was ascribed to supernatural agencies. The fact that an emanation of vital magnetism from one individual may act upon another—just as an emanation from the brain acts upon the fingers—effectually annihilates the miserable superstition in regard to strange, supernatural, and chimerical potencies, by teaching us most impressively to see in ourselves the natural cause of many strange and wierd-like effects. And while magnetism prove this; somnambulism proves the quality of man, by bringing out in bold and undeniable relief the interior mind, independent of the organic functions of sense.

It should be remembered that all somnambulists do not manifest any extraordinary exaltation of ideas; in fact, a large portion who are subject to this state naturally, simply display their ordinary powers of mind. This class generally re-inact their more recent occupations. I know an individual who was a natural somnambule, who, on one occasion, while asleep took the straw from his own bed and bound it into bundles. During the day he had been employed in binding oats, and on this occasion he dreamed he was engaged in the same employment. This individual mind never soared beyond the limits of sensuous perceptions. His waking and sleeping ideas invariably flowed in the same channel; for, according to his own account, his dreams were always perfectly practical ideas, utterly devoid of fantastic imagery or fanciful flights.

The somnambulic manifestations of Miss Susan Packard, of Geneva, N. Y., furnishes a striking contrast to the above, and fully illustrates the opposite extreme. This lady was naturally shy and retiring in her manners, when in an ordinary state. All of her early life had been devoted to service as a "help" in the culinary department of a boarding-house. Her education was supposed to be rather below ordinary. In short, she was looked upon as being extremely commonplace, and no one ever thought of giving her credit for more than a very common degree of intelligence. At the age of fifteen she was prostrated with a severe illness, and it was during her recovery from this that her first somnambulic manifestation occurred. One night the inmates of the house where she was stopping were aroused from their slumber by an unusual manifestation of chanting melody. At first the listeners supposed the beautiful music came from some wandering serenader; but upon investigation it was found that the singing was executed in the room where Susan was sleeping, and at once they proposed to investigate the phenomena. The noise made by the listeners in their endeavors to open the door, awoke her; whereupon she enquired what was wanting. In answer to their enquiry of who had been singing in her room, Susan replied that she had not heard any singing that night; and she was further positive that there had been no music in her room, for there was no one there besides herself, and she had been sound asleep all night. At this the aroused inmates retired, supposing they had been deceived as to the locality from whence the melody had proceeded. But before morning they were again aroused by a repetition of the same melodious chanting; and again following the sound, they traced it to the room occupied by this lady. Some one advanced the idea that Susan, who was the only inmate of the room, might possibly be singing in her sleep; and in accordance with this hint, they proceeded to enter the room as still as possible. On entering, they found the idea fully corroborated, for there lay Susan apparently wrapped in profound and peaceful slumber, singing a beautiful chant, every word and intonation of which was rendered with the same artistic skill that was displayed by the leader of the village choir.

For two years following this time this lady was almost nightly subject to somnambulic manifestations. At times she would sing, and at others she would engage in oratorical delivery; and on one occasion she was discovered reënacting a tragic scene she had a short time before witnessed at a theatrical performance.

There was something remarkable in these sleeping

performances of Susan Packard. Her ideas appeared to be elevated; still she never undertook to do anything different from what she had seen others do. She sang the most difficult pieces performed by the village choir, but in no instance did she undertake common music; also her oratorical deliveries were always imitations of the very finest addresses to which she had listened. Evidently she only gave expression to her own innate ideas; for if such had not been the case, she would at times undoubtedly have performed something she had not before heard or witnessed. Still, she performed things of which she was absolutely incapable when in her ordinary condition; and this incapacity was probably owing to the operations of her nervous organism.

I have so far considered somnambulism only as a natural phenomena, merely to show how closely it is allied to the phenomena of hypnotism, or magnetic somnambulism. I do not believe that a natural somnambule ever expresses an idea foreign to his own mind; while at the same time I am forced to admit that they often display most wonderful powers. But I believe that this unusual display of intelligence by somnambules is in consequence of mental emancipation from organic thraldom, instead of any influx of foreign intelligence.

That somnambulism caused by magnetic processes, differs from the natural phenomena sufficiently to cause mediums to be capable of receiving and imparting foreign intelligence, is fully proven by the hypnotic phenomena, so illustrated by Mr. Broid; who by experiment found that persons subject to magnetic somnambulism were susceptible to an increase of intellectual powers while in that condition. Mr. Broid tried his hypnotic experiments on persons of different degrees of intelligence, but invariably found that the normal capacity of a subject made no difference in the result. A girl from one of the work-houses of Manchester (England), who was ignorant of the grammar of her own language when awake, was found when in a condition of magnetic somnambulism to be capable of accompanying any one in singing songs in *any* language, giving both notes and words correctly. This wonderful feat she was altogether incompetent of performing in her natural or waking condition.

On one occasion this girl was tested by the Swedish Nightingale, Jenny Lind, who tried her somnambulic powers to the utmost. Jenny sang a continual strain of the most difficult *roulades* and *cadenzas*, including some of her extraordinary *sostenuto* notes, with all their inflections, from *pianissimo* to *forte-crescendo*; but in all these fantastic tricks and displays of vocal genius she was so closely followed and accurately imitated by the somnambulist, that at times it was impossible to tell, merely by hearing, that there were two individuals singing. Mr. Broid's hypnotized subjects would, when in proper magnetic condition, accurately repeat what another individual was reading in a separate room, word for word, and although they could not hear them, their pronunciation would be simultaneous with the reader, and correspond with their inflections and variations of sound.

Hypnotic somnambulists are simply mediums of foreign intelligence—a sort of spout through which flows ideas emanating from other minds than their own. They have no recollection of what they do or say; nor do their manifestations of intelligence in any way influence their waking thoughts. When under the influence of certain persons they simply reiterate what they express; and during all these performances their nervous system is in a condition of complete dormancy, every sense is inactive, and though they repeat only what is vocally expressed by those under whose control they may at the time be, they appear to make no use of the organs of hearing, while at the same time they are unable to give expression to unuttered thoughts. Apparently the same power that causes vocal expression in the operator by magnetic power sets in motion the vocal organs of the somnambule.

This hypnotic phenomena is in principle synonymous to the somnambulic manifestations of modern spiritual mediums. The medium, who, in a state of unconsciousness, gives utterance to foreign intelligence, is simply a hypnotic somnambulist, and nothing more. They give utterance to the expressed thoughts of an invisible, though actual intelligence, and like the hypnotic subject, they are simply machines, operated by a foreign power. Magnetic somnambulism and the phenomena of hypnotism may be considered as the second degree of human magnetism, or higher phase of magnetic art. No particular difference in fundamental principles is involved in these tried phases of mesmerism; for somnambulism is the natural result of continued induction of a magnetic current. But while the principles are the same, the effects are widely different. For in simple mesmerism the subject loses only the powers of sense; but in this second, or somnambulic degree, he loses not only these, but the conscious powers of mind. Any person who can be thrown into a somnambulic state by a living operator, can become a trance speaker, or hypnotic operator and spiritual medium.

I have said that somnambulism was not clairvoyance; still the two phenomena are closely allied. The mind of the natural somnambule at times, as we have seen, appears to be exalted; while in other instances, where the phenomena has been superinduced by magnetic power, it is like the senses, deadened or reduced to an unconscious and inoperative condition; from which state, if the magnetic current be continued properly, it will enter into the third magnetic degree, which is clairvoyance.

Clairvoyance is a French term, meaning "clear vision," and is by Webster defined as "the power of discerning objects not visible to the senses, by magnetic influence." But while the term implies clear perception of things beyond the power of bodily vision, it does not imply an understanding of the things observed. A passable good clairvoyant may be a ready observer of things, and yet be incapable of rendering a definite description of what he sees. I have known good clairvoyants, with vision perfectly clear, who could see diseases in the human body; who could discern distant objects; and yet their understandings were so undeveloped that they were incapable of denominating the disease, or discovering proper remedies, or even describing the objects which they saw. This fact will not surprise us when we recollect that clairvoyance means simply clear vision, without reference whatever to the state of the understanding. Hence, the reason why some apparently good clairvoyants fail to impart a clear and accurate idea of what they distinctly see, is owing to the limitations of their intellects and descriptive powers. Thus the errors which are often committed by clairvoyants is not owing to a design to deceive on their part, nor influx of deception from evil spirits—which some superstitious sectarians affirm to be the case—but is solely in consequence of a lack of comprehension on the part of the subject. Let the reader remember the independent clairvoyant receives no influx of intelligence from foreign sources—that he relies upon his own natural abilities of comprehension, and that he receives no exaltation of intellectual power, farther than an exaltation of the powers of perception. Keeping these facts in mind, we can easily comprehend the truth, that the clairvoyant state is not one which puts the subject in possession of boundless wisdom, but a condition, properly speaking, in which the mind has a clear vision, independent of the external senses; and that the inferences of the subject is always in proportion to their inate understanding, or interior development of mind.

The phenomena of clairvoyance can be elucidated or philosophically accounted for, by logical conclusions, deduced from the hypothesis of nervous quality alone. If man is not a two-fold being then the phenomena of clairvoyance cannot exist; for if the external organs of sight are the only means of vision, it would be simply impossible for the mind to discern objects when the orbs of sight were obstructed. But if there is a quality of vision, an external and internal power of actual perception, clairvoyance is, to say the least, possible. I think there is no one who will doubt the idea of human quality; for to deny it is synonymous to a denial of spirit existence. If man is not a two-fold being, the organic faculties are the ultra limit of existence; or, in other words, sense and mind are one and the same. But the fact that man has memory and powers of reason, combined with the innate belief of a separate mental existence hereafter, when the external organs of sense shall have mouldered back to their elementary level, clearly demonstrates to every one whose mind is not hampered by the foolish theories of materialism, that man, here in his primary condition, is a dual being, endowed with spiritual and organic powers. Hence, if man is two-fold, it is but common sense to infer that the outer organs of vision, like all the other senses, are but the external forms of interior principles corresponding to them; and that while the eye reflects objects, it is the mind alone that comprehends.

The clairvoyant is bereft of the external powers of vision—that is, the organic faculty of sight has lost its positive and negative principle of equilibrium by magnetic disturbance of the vitalic medium of sensation is perverted. The mind now fully spiritualized or disenthralled, retains all its normal powers of active intellectuality. The mind naturally visually discerns objects by means of the organs of sight; which organs are exactly suited to the convolving circumstances of ordinary life. They are the material senses, and are perfectly adapted to material life, but are inadequate to the spiritual powers of the mind. No sensation of a spiritual nature can penetrate the higher faculties of the mind through these material organs, no more than the air or any etherial element can make a visible impression upon the optic nerves. Clairvoyance sees things with the internal organs of sight as clearly as the mind discerns objects that are reflected upon the organic eye; and this phenomena is in consequence of direct magnetic connection between the object discerned and the spiritual or inner man. The natural eye is but a medium of sight—a sort of material machine or apparatus capable of reflection, or, to use a common phrase, the eye is the "window of the soul." Still, the power of vision does not consist alone in the power of the visual organs, for the eye may reflect without bearing any impression to the mind. There is, in fact, another power besides the reflective capacity of the orbs of vision; and that power is the all-pervading, vitalizing medium of sensation, *magnetism.* Therefore, magnetic connection is the fundamental principle of mental discernment. When the inherent organ of vision is clairvoyant, it is, as I have said, in direct magnetic connection with whatever object is discerned, and the magnetic powers of the mind, the spiritual being, is in sympathy with the same elements existing in other bodies. No person can be a clairvoyant while the organs of sense remain active; for these organs being, as they are, adapted to material wants alone, hold the mind subject to material impressions. But when these organs are sealed by the induction of a positive magnetic force, the mind becomes spiritualized. The soul is then the individual disenthralled power; freed from the demands of sensuous life, it revels in the freedom of magnetic connection, which is the basis or underlying principle of "clear vision." The clairvoyant sees things as we will all see them when our souls are by death freed from the controlling powers of material sense.

No person can become a clairvoyant whose mind is actuated by mercenary designs, for this power is truly natural, and irrevocably opposed to everything that is low, selfish, or evil. Therefore, any person who is susceptible to magnetic somnambulism may become a clairvoyant, providing they seek the condition with a mind perfectly free from mercenary motives. From personal experience I know this to be true; for I never arrived at this condition, this third magnetic degree, when any low, evil, or mercenary object was sought; though I have frequently endeavored to do so.

CHAPTER XVI.

THE DUALITY OF MAN.

BEFORE entering into a consideration of man's spiritual nature and power, it is highly necessary for us to fully comprehend his duality of organization. I have before said that man was a two-fold being; that beside his physical organization he was endowed with a spiritual or divine principle. This spiritual principle is the positive power of the human organism; hence, it is the vitalizing and animating force, as well as the *attracting* power. In a word, the spirit—the soul—the immortal part of man may be considered as the builder of the organic structure. The entire physical organism is perfectly adapted to the conditions and influences of material life. It is constructed with especial adaptations to the rudimental wants of the spirit. In short, the physical organism is simply an encasement of the interior or spiritual principle, and is an organic means of spirit manifestation. Every movement is a manifestation of spirit power and intelligence, as well as interior life. The breath of life is not in the spirit or soul; for the soul is the germ of divinity. Nor is the physical organism an independent living principle. God made *man* of the dust of the ground, then breathed into his nostrils the breath of life, and man *became* a living soul. According to this account of Moses, in regard to the creation of man, we see that God did not create the life principle out of the dust of the ground. He only created the physical organism, and into this he breathed the breath of life, by which act "man became a living soul." Here the duality of man is illustrated; for in Adam the physical man was combined with a vitalizing principle of life, and this life principle became a living soul or spirit.

I cannot imagine how any man can suppose that the physical organism, and the life principle are the same; and at the same time entertain a belief in future existence; for, if the physical man is the basis of animate existence, it certainly must be the supreme power of life; and if it is the supreme power of rudimental life, it is subject to death, on the occasion of physical dissolution, for organic perfection is necessary to organic life. Do not misconstrue my meaning. There are many able investigators who believe that the physical organism is the creative power, the positive force, and that the mind or spirit is the offspring of sense; hence, negative to the organic functions. Now, I hold, if this is the case, a physical organization is necessary to the existence of a spirit; hence, at physical death the mind or spirit must die.

But this theory of organic superiority is not only absurd, but is unsupported. The phenomena of human psychology proves beyond a doubt, that the mind, will, or spirit, is the positive power in the human organism. Every well informed individual is familiar with the influence of the mind upon the body in disease. Whenever a fatal epidemic prevails in a community it is not an uncommon thing to see impressible persons psychologized by fear. I believe that I speak the truth, when I say that one-half of the victims of the Asiatic cholera, die solely in consequence of psychological influence. In these instances fear disturbs the proper equilibrium of the mind. One faculty—that is the faculty of fear—absorbs all the powers of the mind; every other faculty is morbidly inactive. There is no power to combat the epidemic. The organ of combativeness is robbed of the vitalizing medium by the organ of fear; and thus, an avenue is thrown wide open to the admission and possession of the enemy. The poet Wordsworth, in his poem of Goody Blake, and Harry Gill, gives a good illustration of psychological action of mind upon the body. Poor Goody, the stern, hard-hearted, Harry Gill might never again be warm. This simple prayer had a powerful psychological effect upon Harry's poor superstitious mind. The next day, he complained of being cold; and although he covered himself with many blankets, still he could not get warm; and all this dreadful array of suffering was in consequence of one psychological impression. For fear of cold air, this man kept his bed for twenty years, and at last died a victim to this one insanse idea.

The whole secret of this horrid effect is revealed when we comprehend the psychological power of the human mind.

In psychology, every thing that disturbs the equilibrium of the mental forces is capable of destroying the unity of mental action; and when this unity is destroyed some one faculty preponderates over all the other. Thus—when fear has gained a preponderance of power over the other faculties of the mind, that faculty is, for the time being, the supreme motive power. Every physical manifestation reveals what power of mind is in the ascendancy. If it is fear, or caution, that preponderates, we behold a trembling, cringing, physical demonstration of fright. If the organ of combativeness holds the balance of power, we see a blustering demonstration of bravado. And so there is a physical demonstration for all the varying phases of the human mind. These external manifestations, ever varying, as they are, prove that there is an internal force, or internal power, which is independant of the organic function. This power we term spirit, and by this term we mean, the life principle, the immortal part, the reasoning, thinking, comprehending, and animating portion of the human organism. This principle is also the positive force and the controling agent. The physical organism is the slave of the mind, or spirit; for every voluntary motion is the result of spirit power. It is by the power of the spirit that we accomplish muscular action. Hence, the spirit is the cause, and the physical organism the means of manifestation. Still the spirit may act without making any material or physical demonstration. We may think without manifesting our thoughts, but we cannot make a voluntary muscular movement without the aid of the will power. Thus we conclude, that the dualty of man, consist of man physical, and man spiritual. The first, is the material organism; the last, is the divine principle. The physical man is of the earth, earthy. The spiritual man is the animating, controling, vitalizing, interior life principle.

If man is a two-fold being, endowed with a positive, spirit power, which controls the organism, or physical man, that spirit must be an identified principle, and if it is an identified principle, capable of in dependent action; and we may reasonably suppose its identified or individual existence to be eternal. Farther, if it is the positive controling power of the material organism, that power is as much a power, in one sphere of existence as in another.

If these positions are correct, then the phenomena of modern spirit manifestations can be philosophically accounted for. But if the reverse conclusion is correct, that is, if the physical organism is the cause of physical manifestation, or controling power, then the whole phenomena is simply delusion; for we all know that after death the body is an inactive mass of material, utterly devoid of intelligence.

I hold that the former proposition is correct; and shall from that stand-point, proceed to illustrate the phenomena of modern spiritualism.

Taking it for granted that my readers believe in the immortality of the spirit, or eternal identified existance of the life principle, I will at once enter upon a consideration of spirit power.

Remembering the duality of man; let us investigate the means employed by the spirit to produce the phenomena of muscular action; while, in rudimental connection with the body; which is the first sphere of spirit existence.

To move one's hand is a simple act; but how the hand is moved by the will power of the spirit, is a question of great importance; for it involves the whole phenomena of spirit's rudimental or primary powers.

I have, in one of the preceeding chapters, stated that I believe the brain to be a resorvoir of electric forces, and that this electric force was generated by the chemical action of the blood. Evidently this generated electricity is the agent of the mind, and instrument of spirit power; or rather, this electric fluid is the medium between the immortal and divine principle and the material organism. When the mind wills the hand to move, the brain—which may be considered as the body-servant of the mind—throws its concentrated, electric force into the muscles of the arm in a quantity just sufficient to accomplish the movement commanded by the superior power. The first cause of every voluntary muscular movement has its origin in the supreme or spirit power. The means to accomplish this muscular movement, has its origin in the brain; and the means or agent which I have said was generated by the brain from the electric properties of the blood, is doubtless some modification of the well known element, electricity.

From the above it will be seen that the spirit in order to produce the phenomena of muscular motion, must necessary bring into requisition some material element. If the brain was robbed of its chemical powers, or denied its quota of blood; or if the blood was despoiled of its electric producing constituents, the divine principle or will would have no means of action. Still, this robbing it of material means of manifestation would in no way destroy its innate powers of action, no more than the severing of a telegraphic wire would destroy the innate power of a voltaic battery. The spirit is an independent principle, so far as existence is concerned; but is dependent upon material organism for the means of manifesting that existence. Without the spirit, the physical organism of man is a mass of inert material. The physical organs have no force or spring of action within themselves, but derive all their energies from some external force. No single organ, or function, is self-acting. It must be set in action by influences outside of itself. Thus the lungs, perfect in their structure, cannot act without the air. The delicately constructed ear, cannot perform its function without the necessary vibration of the atmosphere. Nor is the brain any more self-acting than any other organ; for like the others it requires an agent outside of itself;

and that agent is electricity, or some modification of that element. The brain, like all other organs of use, is but material substance, and is the operative means of spirit manifestation. The brain is not the spirit, nor is it the direct medium between the finite and the infinite, the spiritual and physical; but is simply the power that collects and arranges the material which is the vehicle of thought, sensation, and intelligence. The particles of matter of which the brain is composed may be weighed, tested, analyzed, tortured in a thousand ways; but no observation from the outside will ever reveal the mystery of spirit power, or comprehend the essence of mind. We may analyze the brain and determine its function; but the infinite spirit, the great positive power of human existence is still beyond our comprehension. We can know the attributes of mind only by its outward or material manifestation. We have no means of ascertaining whether it be material or immaterial; to us the spirit must ever be considered a principle.

But though we cannot analyze the spirit, or even determine its structure, we can comprehend its means of manifestation; for these means are material in their nature, and are therefore capable of analytic comprehension.

CHAPTER XVII.

SPIRIT MEANS OF PHYSICAL CONTROL.

I HAVE in the preceding chapter, considered the spirit as the positive, controlling power. It is likewise the organizing power and permanent individual principle of eternal identified existence. Organized matter, cannot, from its nature, be presistent. But the power—which is the spirit—that organizes and re-organizes the physical structure is alone permanent.

In the human structure the organizing life-force or spirit is co-equal to the death action, and by its power we preserve our bodily form and physical identity through a long series of years. But this identity of matter, as a body, does not constitute identity of person; for health is continuously undergoing change. The material of our bodies, though ours to-day, may to-morrow, be in part the slave of another individual spirit or organic force. Hence, in speaking of human identity, I do not refer to the material organism, or physical form; but to the organizing force that lies back of organization itself. It is this force which constitutes individual identity; for it is the self of existence and primary cause of material form. In short, as I have before said, the spirit is the real man; the physical organism being only a material means of spirit manifestation, adapted to material wants.

The great Apostle alludes to this scientific truth when teaching the sublime doctrine of the resurrection of the dead. In answer to the momentous question, how are the dead raised? and, with what body do they come? He taught: that the identity of matter did not constitute the identity of man; but that there was back of the material organism, an individual, self-conscious, invisible life-force; which was a real, identified, eternally existing principle!

We have seen that the spirit or organizing force is in material life, or primary existence, the positive cause of material action; and that this power is innate force or underived capability. Yet, like the spirit or principle of power, is in the body; it cannot manifest existence only by bringing into requisition a material element as a medium or means of demonstration. That element, we have considered as being some modification of electricity.

We may reasonably suppose that disembodied spirits retain all the power of spirits in the body; for if they are the positive or organizing and manifesting power in the body, they must be, when disembodied, or else in some way be dependent upon matter for power as well as means to act; and if we admit this, we deny the absolute identity of the spirit; and in reality prove ourselves to be simply materialists, for like them we admit the spirit to be nothing but a concentration of refined material forces, whose very existence depends upon the existence of the physical organism.

Taking it for granted that my readers believe in the immortality of the spirit, and that the spirit or life principle is the positive cause of material manifestation and real principal of existence, while in the body; I will at once enter into a consideration of the phenomena of modern Spritualism.

Disembodied spirit manifestation first attracted public attention at Hydesville, N. Y., in 1848; and there first demonstrations consisted of "raps," or rather electric sounds; which were apparently caused by some mysterious agency, through the mediumship of certain members of the Fox family. Since that date, the phenomena known as the "raps," has become a powerful means of spirit communication, as well, as the basis of a world revolutionizing philosophy. Still, to many individuals, these simple "raps" are but an astounding effect of some hidden and mysterious causes, beyond the comprehension of material sense or worldly reason. Many recognize them as the material manifestations of spirit power; yet, are unable to determine in what manner they are produced. To these, the question often arises—"upon what principles or conditions are spiritual communications made?"—and how are these manifestations accomplished? To the first query, investigation enables me to reply, that a good moral or intellectual state is not a prerequisite condition on the part of the individual or individuals who constitute the mediums, for electrical intercourse with disembodied spirits by means of the "raps" This, at the first glance, seems a strange inconsistency. But when we consider that the spirits who communicate to the earth's inhabitants in this electrial manner, do not, as a general principle, allow their thoughts to flow into the mind of the medium, and thence by pronunciation to the individual with whom they discourse; but, on the contrary, that the spirits impart what they desire to communicate through electrical vibrations alphabetically. I say, when we consider all this, it ceases to be a mysterious inconsistency, that good moral and intellectual conditions are not required. If these spiritual communications were made through the minds of mediums, as through spiritually illuminated seers, prophets, and clairvoyants, then constitutional harmony, combined with fine moral and intellectual tendencies, would be the indispensible conditions; but as these manifestations of material control are not conducted through the mediatorial agency of the mind, we must necessarily conclude, that as far as the medium (or person) is concerned, some physical condition is alone required. This supposition is correct.

We have seen—and I think no one will doubt the position—that the spirit, or mind, manifests power and intelligence while in the body, by means of an electric fluid; which, as an element, is so refined and antenuated, that the most exquisitely constructed electro-meter is incapable of detecting its presence. It is but common sense to infer, that if the spirit employs a material substance as an agent of material manifestation while in the body, that it would employ the same agent to manifest power when disembodied. Hence, in order for a person to become a spiritual medium, it is necessary that there should be an emanation of vital electricity from their physical organism, in a quantity sufficient not only to perform the function of their own mind; but, at the same time form a connection, electrical, between their organism, and the controlling disembodied spirit power. I have concluded, after much investigation, of the phenomena of spirit intercourse, that the *means* of communication all emanate from the medium. That is, that the medium is the battery, that furnishes the electric connection; for, if such was not the case, I can see no reason why disembodied spirits could not manifest intelligence, without a medium as well as with; nor why they cannot communicate through one individual as well as another.

We now come to a consideration of the second inquiry, which is, how do disembodied spirits communicate with man in his primary condition? As I have only referred to one species of manifestations, namely —the phenomena of the "raps"— I will confine myself to an elucidation of those mysterious manifestations of spirit power. The principles involved in these demonstrations are simple, and physical, philosophical, and rational; because they are no more wonderful or complicated than the principles upon which the magnetic telegraph is daily operating along our great commercial avenues. In fact, the principle involved in both phenomenas, are alike ; and there is even a similarity in the two elementary agents employed. We all know that electricity is the transmitting agent in all telegraph operations ; or, in other words, electricity is in the art of magnetic telegraphing employed as a vehicle of intelligence. No communication can be transmitted until there is an electric connection between the point of recieving intelligence and the place from whence the intelligence emanates; and this connection must consist of a continuous thread of electric fluid. The fact that there is a material connection between two points by means of a wire or cable, is no sign that there is a natural electric connection of power sufficient to transmit intelligence, or even electric sound. This power, or rather this continuous line of electric fluid, must be superinduced by bringing into requisition the decomposing powers of a voltaic battery ; hence we conclude that the real vehicle of power in telegraphing is an electric current, foreign to that contained in the wire when in normal condition. The wire is simply a means of support—a material pathway, along which this more refined element is extended—capable of retaining the induced current in an unbroken chain from one terminus to the other, and this electric current is the real medium employed in magnetic telegraphing.

In the phenomena of material manifestation by

spirits, the same principles are involved. Apollos Munn, who was deep in the philosophy of spirit intercourse by electrical sounds, says:

"In order to perceive the analogy between the spiritual and the natural worlds by electrical rappings, and the mode of communicating between distant places by magnetic telegraph, let it first be understood that each created thing sustains certain electrical relations to all other things; that all higher forms of development sustain positive relations to all lower forms—as the vegetable to the mineral, the animal to the vegetable, and *man* to all the lower kingdoms in nature. Ascending still further in the scale of progression, the rule will hold good; and hence it is evident that the spirit world sustains a positive electrical relation to the natural world, of which it is a higher form—a further and more perfect development. When spirits leave the body the transition causes them no loss of intelligence or power. On the contrary, as every step in their history while, in the body, is marked by that law of progression which developes knowledge and power in exact ratio with the refinement of the spirit, it is reasonable to suppose that their power over the refined elements in nature, and their knowledge of the laws that govern them, will be greatly increased by their immediate assimilation with the refinement and knowledge which pervade the second sphere of human existence. They cannot, it is true, come in immediate contact with gross substances, but they can, and do, act upon them with powerful effect through the agency of magnetism and electricity. Thus, it cannot be disputed, admitting that the spirit progresses hereafter, that the inhabitants of the spirit-world have the power, when natural conditions are complied with, to communicate electricity with their friends in the body. When nature, by her constant movement toward the refinement of matter, developes mediums through whom communications can be made, the spirits will be found ready to respond to our desires. These mediums are sometimes furnished by certain localities, usually designated as "haunted houses," where the electricity from certain causes has become so rare and refined that spirits can there manifest their power and presence in various ways. The young ladies of the Fox family, and hundreds of other individuals through whom spirits communicate, are mediums, because the electrical atmosphere which emanates from their systems contains but little gross electricity. The spirits sustaining positive relations to us are enabled through these mediums or conductors to attract and move articles of furniture, vibrate the wires of a musical instrument, and by discharging, by the power of their will, currents of magnetism, they can, and do produce rappings, like the magnetic telegraph, corresponding to letters of the alphabet."

Vital electricity is, without doubt, the prominent agent employed by spirits in producing the phenomena of electric sounds, and this agent, as I have said, emanates from the medium. A spirit, though it does not possess any of the grossness of the earthly form, is yet an organized power, with functions precisely like those possessed by the spirit in the body; and when it desires to produce a manifestation it brings its own magnetic and positive powers in electric connection with the vital electricity emanating from the medium. When the connection has been formed the spirit by its will power causes electrical concussions upon some material substance, through the intermediate agencies of spirit magnetism and organic electricity.

The *modus operandi* of those phenomena is in detail beyond present investigation; but that spirits do come in contact or rapport with organic and material substances through electrical agencies, is proven by every man's experience. Being the self of existence, it is the spirit alone that thinks, feels, loves, and reasons; by its power railroads and steamboats are made and managed; it is by the power of the spirit through the mediumship of vital electricity that every kind of labor is performed. If you desire to lift a certain weight, it is the spirit or will power that sets in operation the various organic agencies natural to the physical organism. The first of the agents is vital electricity, the second, spirit magnetism, the third, the nervous structure, the fourth, the physical muscles, and the fifth is the bones, which by acting in concert with the other named agents, succeeds in raising the weight. Each and all of these agents are powerless to perform an act, unless managed, controlled and set in operation by the spirit or interior power. When disembodied spirits find a person whose mind is sufficiently passive, and who is a conductor of vital electricity—which is the primary agent—they can produce to a limited extent, results like those produced by the spirit while in the body.

There are but few individuals in the United States at the present time that are not personally acquainted with persons who are spirit electric mediums, and through them they have witnessed some phase of electric manifestation, such as the raps, table-tipping, or some other material demonstration; and these individuals know full well that the majority of these manifestations are emanations from some power gifted with intelligence. But the question arises,—what proof is there that these novel expressions of intelligence do not emanate from local agencies? Now this is an exceedingly difficult query to answer satisfactorily. Still, there is *logical* proof that these manifestations do come from spirits, or some source other than immediate local agencies. All purported spirit communications are found, on enquiry, to be claimed by disembodied spirits, who announce themselves to be identified powers of intelligence. Now if these communications, which are invariably claimed as emanations of spirit knowledge, are in reality but emanations of intelligence, imperceptibly and unconsciously flowing from the minds of individuals who may be in magnetic relation with the medium through which the intelligence flows; I say, if such is the case, I can see no philosophical reason why the communication should purport to come from spirits, for it is reasonable to infer that the same power that could imperceptibly and unconsciously impart an intelligent idea by electric sounds alphabetically would, with equal unconsciousness of act, claim authorship. Beside this, there are other reasons for doubting the idea that these manifestations of intelligence proceed from the human mind. Often communications are received which are in direct opposition to all the preconceived ideas entertained by those who happen to be in magnetic rapport with the medium of intelligence; hence if these communications come from the minds of those who are in magnetic connection with the medium, they must, of necessity, be imperceptible ideas. But here we find ourselves engaged in combat with an undeniable truth; for it is utterly impossible for a man to be in possession of an idea or thought, and at the same time, while in normal condition, be unconscious of such possession; but even if we admit that he could unconsciously possess a thought, still we are no better off; for he certainly could not give expression to a thought in language, without being conscious of the thought at the time of utterance, for we all know that it is impossible for an individual to express an idea, either vocally or otherwise, until after such idea has been mentally arranged. Therefore, if these material manifestations of intelligence are not imperceptible ideas emanating from the human mind, they must be, either the offspring of spirit intelligence or preconceived ideas perceptibly emanating from some individual human organism, or local fountain of intelligence. If the latter supposition is correct there could be no intelligence imparted by electrical sound that was not already a recognized idea by at least one member of a magnetic circle.

My own personal experience proves this supposition to be an absurdity. The reader will remember that I am daily influenced by an Indian Doctor, and that it is not an uncommon occurrence for him to express his ideas in his native language through me as a medium. (This phenomena has been repeatedly tested by competent persons who understood the language spoken, hence I confidently assert that I do, when in a condition of somnambulism, speak in the Indian dialect.) Not one of a thousand who hear me talking this language understands a single word of what I express; nor can I when in a normal condition speak half a dozen words in the Indian tongue. Still there is hardly a day but what I talk more or less in this dialect when under influence, and that too when there is no possibility of there being a magnetic connection between myself as a medium, and any individual understanding the Indian language. In this case, local emanation of intelligence is literally impossible; hence it becomes necessary for us to look elsewhere for a cause of the effect.

These communications claim to emanate from the identified spirit of an Indian, and as they are decidedly Indian in their character, the claim is, to say the least, worthy of consideration. Besides, to what other power can we attribute them? We cannot say that it is a concentration of chaotic or disorganized intelligence, floating in the atmosphere, because all intelligence is simply a manifestation of spirit power. Disorganized intelligence is an absurdity—a supposed something that really does not exist—in fact, cannot exist independent of the spirit, no more than sunlight can exist independent of the sun.

I think that no one who will impartially investigate the phenomena of spirit communications will fail to recognize them as manifestations of spirit power; for it is the only philosophical elucidation of the mystery that does not clash with logical reasonings.

CHAPTER XVIII.

HOW SPIRITS COMMUNICATE.

IN PURSUING our investigation of the subject of spirit communication, we must remember that all manifestations of spirit power and intelligence depends for means of accomplishment upon vital electricity alone; and that this is an imperative means or auxilliary of spirit power, whether embodied or disembodied, to manifest identity.

We may think, but we cannot make our thoughts known without bringing into requisition this material agent. Disembodied spirits may, through sympathy, manifest their intelligence to one another without bringing to their aid this element; but without it they can make no material demonstration. We in the body can think, but the moment we manifest our thoughts—whether by speaking, by writing, or by pantomimic action—we are forced to bring into requisition this material element as a medium of power. Hence, we conclude that all spirit manifestation or material demonstration of spirit intelligence, are dependent upon this same agent for means of accomplishment. We have considered the raps to be simply electric vibrations caused by the will power of disembodied spirits, operating upon a current of vital electricity emanating from the physical organism of the medium. But this simple phase of spirit demonstration does not comprehend the extent of spirit modes of manifestation. Still every different phase is dependent upon this one element for means. All material spirit manifestations, such as the "raps," table-tipping, playing on musical instruments; as well as the mystic phenomena displayed by spirits by means of metallic rings, or by tying and untying difficult entanglements of strings, ropes, etc., are, in fact, but different phases of the same power. In either manifestation the whole means employed is the natural product of the medium; the spirits merely operate through the vital electricity which naturally emanates from the physical organism of the medium alone—providing that the mediums during the manifestations retain their normal powers of mind. But when the medium loses self-consciousness and becomes somnambulic he is simply a conductor of electricity emanating from surrounding bodies.

We have seen in our investigation of somnambulism that magnetic coma was the result of stupefaction of organic sense, superinduced by a continual induction of vital electricity, and that when the physical organism was in this forced condition, the subject's mind was incapable of action or organic demonstration of power, and that the physical organism of a hypnotized subject was subject to the will power of a separate or organically disconnected mind. The question now arises—How can a spirit or mind manifest its power or its intelligence through a separate or organically disconnected organism?

Before entering into a discussion of this phenomena, let me repeat a former assertion, which is that the manifestations of hypnotized subjects is in principle synonymous to the somnambulic manifestations of modern spiritual mediums. Mediums who, in a condition of magnetic unconsciousness, give utterance to foreign intelligence, are simply hypnotic somnambulists, who are hypnotized, not by spirits, but by voluntary absorption of vital electricity. I am aware that many suppose that somnambulic spirit mediums (meaning by this term those mediums who, while they are instruments of spirit power, are magnetically rendered unconscious,) are magnetized by spirits—that is, that the element which causes magnetic coma emanates wholly from them. This idea I consider to be utterly incorrect, from the simple fact that it does not correspond to imperative rules of medial development. The advanced investigator of medial powers knows full well that development depends wholly upon material auxilliaries. Hence the necessity of circles and other material appurtenances. These material substances are inevitable perquisites to medial development, and without them a person cannot become an unconscious or hypnotized spirit medium, and the reason why they cannot is because the power to produce magnetic sleep emanates alone from surrounding material organizations.

A person who designs to become a somnambulic medium of spirit intelligence, must, of an imperative necessity, be naturally a conductor of vital electricity.

All material organizations when in natural condition emit a current of electric fluid; but bodies which are undergoing decomposition throw off by far greater quantities of vital electricity than do bodies undergoing the natural organic changes of life. Also, beings of intelligence can, by the will power of the spirit, increase the volume of electricity beyond its natural or unforced emanation. All emanations of this vital fluid, when thrown from one body immediately seek to cause or effect an equilibrium elsewhere; and for this purpose certain properties, and even persons, are used as conductors. Thus, an individual who is a natural conductor, or even absorbent, of electric fluid, becomes a center or magnetic focus upon which all immediate emanations or exhalations of vital electricity concentrate. Now if the will power of such individual is brought to a passive condition, so as not to exert a counteracting influence, this continued concentration of electric fluid will naturally produce magnetic slumber; for this power or element is, as I have repeatedly asserted, the direct agent of the mind, and is only exhausted through the activity of the mental powers. Hence, during the cessation of mental operations this element, which is positive to all other functions of the physical organism, hold the organic functions in subjection. But, you ask, how can the mind of a medium be rendered inoperative by this agent of the mind? I answer, by destroying the equilibrium naturally existing between the two. We all know that the mind is naturally the positive power, and that it controls with perfect ease every action of the muscular organism. We move the hand by means of this vital electricity governed by the will power of the spirit. In this phenomena the spirit is the positive power, and the electric fluid, which is the means, is the negative; and between them there exists a perfect equilibrium, or positive and negative adaptation to material exigencies. Now were we to introduce a powerful increase of electricity by means of a chemical battery, the relative position of the two powers would be changed, the mind would be the negative, and the vital electricity the positive; and while the two powers were in this condition the mind could neither produce nor prohibit muscular motion, and if there was any such demonstration it would be the direct result of some foreign power.

One has only to take hold of the poles of any ordinary electrical machine when in operation, to fully comprehend this phenomena of reversion of powers, and those who may have experienced an artificial induction of electricity know that the portion of physical organism artificially charged with foreign electricity, is, for the time being, or during such induction ungovernable by the will power of their own mind.

Artificial introduction of a powerful current of electricity causes involuntary contraction and expansion of cords and muscles in the same manner that the mind causes the same phenomena, through the agency of the vital electricity generated by the brain. But while the means to produce the phenomena are in both cases al ke, the manifest appearances of the result are widely different. Motion caused by the will power of the spirit is—except in cases of insanity—a controlled manifestation of intelligence but all other physical movements, caused by electric power, are simply manifestations of power, perfectly aimless and devoid of intelligent limitation or result; and their very aimlessness and fantastic appearances is proof of their positiveness to the will power of the spirit.

Thus, in consideration of these electric phenomena we may reasonably infer that the spirit, which is naturally the positive power, may, by the superior power existing in quantity over nature's limit, be forced into a negative position to vital electricity, which by this increase in quantity, becomes the positive.

Having comprehended the possibility of the will power becoming negative to its natural agent of manifestation—vital electricity, we are prepared to continue our investigation of the phenomena of spiritualism, as displayed by somnambulic mediums.

I have said that there is from all bodies a continuous emanation of vital electricity, which, when thrown from one body, seeks to effect an equilibrium elsewhere, and that certain bodies and even persons were natural conductors of this fluid.

We have no means of ascertaining the exact amount of vital electricity that the human organism is capable of absorbing. Still we are positive that this element of power in the physical organization is subject to natural exhaustion, and if it is naturally liable to exhaustion or decrease in quantity, we may reasonably infer that there is a natural process of recuperation. In fact, we may reasonably assert that the human organism is subject to ever-varying supplies of this element. We all know that continued physical activity causes, not only muscular fatigue, but exhaustion of force to act. Now the force which is thus exhausted by long continued activity, is none other than the immediate agent of the will power, and the primary material cause of physical movement. Every movement of the hand, every word vocally uttered—in short, every voluntary physical action causes a decrease in the quantity of vital electricity generated by the brain, which is, as I have before stated, the natural reservoir of this power. Hence, we conclude the will power or spirit, to be the first or primary cause of electric exhaustion. We are positive that, during mental and physical quietude, this exhaustion of vital force ceases; and in view of the fact that the human organism recovers its exhausted force of powers by rest or inactivity, we logically infer that the physical organism undergoes a process of vitalic recuperation. Therefore, the human organism may be considered as being alternately attractive and repulsive to this vitalic element of power. When the mind ceases its manifestations by outward or physical action, the physical organism becomes a magnet, which attracts from other organisms their ejections of vital electricity. Thus we see why it is necessary for persons who desire magnetic influence to become not only mentally passive, but physically quiet.

There are various ways and means employed by mediums in producing the phenomena of magnetic somnambulism; but there is no process by which it can be produced without the subject or medium coming in contact organically, with some electric producing organization. The idea that an individual can by his own will power, enter into a magnetic condition of unconsciousness, is perfectly erroneous. As well might we argue that one can, by a simple exertion of the will power, cause his own physical death, or stop the circulation of blood in some one portion of his physical organization. The will or spirit has no other duty to perform in producing magnetic slumber than it has in producing ordinary sleep. In either case the mind has only to become passive and allow the physical organism to become quiet.

Some mediums require more electric power to produce magnetic slumber than do others. I have known individuals who could not enter into this unconscious state without the assistance of a powerful magnetizer; others of my acquaintance are obliged to always sit in circles of certain electric power, in order to receive influence; and there is still another class of mediums who have only to rest their hands upon some organic substance, in order to be bourne into this mystic slumber.

These variations are in consequence of a difference in the physical conditions of the subjects. A person with a super-amount of animal life, combined with a restless spirit, must not expect to easily become a magnetic somnambulist, for such an individual—though they may be a magnet to vital electricity—will resist the influence by an almost unconscious operation of the mind. Restless minds are hard to subdue in any case, but when they are continually manifesting their restlessness through the physical organisms, as in cases of nervous temperament, it is next to impossible for even the most powerful magnetizer to cause upon such organisms any magnetic effect.

All persons, when somnambulists, are rendered unconscious by an induction of vital electricity emanating from some contignous material organization, or combination of organic bodies. The productive power in every instance is the same; but at the same time there may be distinct emanations. Thus one individual who is easily influenced, may be magnetized bv simply resting their hands upon a common table, or any other organic body which is undergoing decomposition, or they may be placed in the same condition by an intelligent manipulating process, or by grasping a magnetic cord. In short, there are various ways to produce this effect, but in every instance of magnetic somnambulism, organic connection between the subject and the organic universe is an imperative necessity. I have found by experiment that when a somnambulic medium was completely insulated from organic connection that it was impossible for them to receive a magnetic influence; and it is in view of this fact that I conclude that the means of spirits' manifestation of intelligence are wholly the product of organic electricity, and that disembodied spirits are of themselves incapable of causing magnetic coma.

But you ask how—if spirits do not cause the magnetic influence they can communicate through a hypnotized or somnambulic medium? I have in another chapter of this work, referred to the phenomena of hypnotic somnambulism as demonstrated by Mr. Braid, and the reader will remember that one of his subjects was, on one occasion, under the intelligent control of Jenny Lind. This subject, at this time was neither hyptonized by Jenny nor by Mr. Braid, but was (according to an article published at the time, in the Manchester Courier,) rendered somnambulic in the same manner that thousands of spirit mediums are at the present day, namely: by resting her hands upon a center-table, and at the same time concentrating her gaze upon a piece of silver lying before her. In this case the magnetic power—which caused the subject to become unconscious—emanated from inanimate material organisms; while the manifestation of intelligence come from a distinctly different source. Now there is but one intelligent way to account for this phenomena in a reasonable manner. This subject was magnetized before the manifestation commenced, and even after the manifestation ceased she—the somnambulist—remained unconscious, or under magnetic influence. No part of the element causing this sleep could be supposed to emanate from Miss Lind; but the intelligence manifested undoubtedly did. The subject sang when she sang, and as an accompanist, gave both notes and words simultaneously with her. Evidently the will power of the Swedish Nightingale caused the vocal organs of the subject to act in imitation of her own, through the means of vital electricity. The medium had been magnetized by a voluntary absorption of vital electricity, emanating from contiguous organizations. Her mind had from voluntary passiveness, been reduced to a negative position by a continued induction of electric power, and had thereby lost its operative or organic controlling force, and this result was simply in consequence of the vital electricity of the brain being overpowered by an induction of the same element from other sources.

But notwithstanding her own mind was rendered incapable of causing her own organs to act; those organs did act, and their actions were manifestations of intelligence, and the intelligence which was manifested was the product of the intelligent mind of Jenny Lind, who was organically a separate and distinctly identified being.

Now comes the question—how did the Swedish Nightingale manifest her intelligence through this separate organism? I answer, by means of an electric connection between her mind or spirit, and the magnetized physical organs of the subject, in a manner corresponding to the process of mechanical electric telegraphing. The connection was formed by the will power of Jenny Lind. Her spirit was the magnet. She earnestly desired to test the somnambulic powers of this medium, and that desire caused her mind to be positive to the entire electric power concentrated upon the subject; and, as all positive powers attract their negatives, her mind, being the positive, attracted the negative, or vital electricity, from the physical organization of the subject to her own organism. All the other minds, or identified intelligences in that assembly, on that occasion, were in unison with hers, for they all desired to witness the manifestation. Had this harmony not existed, or, in other words, had there been a confliction of powers, or contrary desires of equal force exerted by those present, there would have been no manifestation through the medium, for there would have been two distinct electric connections, and two distinct operative powers, with only one set of organs to operate through.

I speak of this to show the imperative necessity of complete harmony among individuals who may congregate for the purpose of testing this, or the pheuomena of spirit communication. Where two, or more, electric connections formed between a medium and designing to communicate by pronunciation, the result would be like what would follow in case of a concentration of distinct messages, of different natures, upon one telegraphic apparatus at the same time. One message would be so intermingled with the other, that the whole would be rendered unintelligible.

After a perfect electric connection has been formed between a medium and a spirit designing to communicate, the phenomena of the manifestation is no more complicated or wonderful, than the phenomena of physical manifestation of human intelligence. While the spirit is connected with the body in the earth-life, it demonstrates thought by means of an electric connection, and it is by the same means that disembodied spirits cause material demonstration of intelligence through the organs of hypnotic mediums.

We, in the form, are beings of sympathy; but this sympathy is not the result of physical consanguinity, but of spirit affinity. We may be attracted by a physical form, or at least suppose that therein lies the means of awakening our sympathy; but were we to closely investigate the cause of our being thus attracted, we would find that the real power or first cause of our sympathy emanated from the spirit enshrined in the body. Hence, sympathy, being a concomitant of the spirit, we infer that it is a principle as eternal in existence as is the spirit. Love, sociability, and kindly regard are the offspring of spirit sympathy, and the more intelligent and refined the spirit is, the more fervent are these adjuncts of the principle of mental sympathetic consanguinity. Sympathy creates a desire for reciprocal exchange of sentiment, and thereby man becomes a social being. We love, because in the object of our love, our spirit finds its affinity, and affinities will inevitably seek to commingle with one another; hence, so long as sentiments are in affinity between mind and mind, so long a desire for sympathetic intercourse will remain, and though one mind may be in the realms of spirits, the desire will still exist. I am aware that many believe that the spirit when freed from the thraldom of the physical form, loses its sympathy for things terrestrial; but if such is the case, then the spirit at death loses its identity, or rather its individuality. We know the man by his outward form; but we know the spirit by its manifestations alone. We cannot see it, even with our mind's eye; hence, if its manifestations are entirely changed in the spirit world, its identity to *us* must be certainly *lost.* But if its manifestations are unchanged, its power to cause manifestations must remain, and not only its powers, but its desire, remains to demonstrate to its former friends its unchanged sympathy and affinity of thought and affection. Will the affectionate wife believe that her dearly loved bosom companion who has gone before her to the fadeless "summer-land," has ceased to appreciate the holy bond of spirit sympathy, that through life made them as one in sentiment? No! her whole nature revolts at the bare supposition of such an unnatural result. What is life without spirit affinity? Nothing but an empty, meaningless farce. What use would there be for cultivating the holy aspirations of the soul, if those aspirations are to be lost when we pass beyond the confines of mortal life? I answer, none. If the spirit on the event of physical death, undergoes such a change that it loses its affinity for, and sympathy with the things appertaining to this life, then all the plans of salvation are delusions, and all moral requirements are fictitious absurdities. In short, if the spirit is robbed of all its earthly characteristics, when separated from the body by what we term death, it is no longer the same spirit, but a new one no way like the old. But if it is the same spirit in the celestial realms, that once animated a form of clay, that spirit must retain all its innate powers for material manifestation that characterized it while in the body; hence, when it comes in contact with the means which nature has adapted to its use, it can communicate its intelligence with the same ease it could while in the body.

The spirit, while in the body, usually communicates its thoughts through the instrumentality of the vocal organs. A portion of the powers necessary to vocal utterance are furnished by the involuntary forces of our nature, and over these the spirit has no control. The air inhaled and exhaled by the lungs is one means of vocal expression, a proper development of the organs of speech is another; but, though there exists these perfect qualifications, the result or manifestation of intelligence depends wholly upon the power of the mind to produce regulated sound; and the spirit causes such sound by means of vital electricity—in something the same manner that the magnetic telegraph operator produces an intelligent sound upon a distant electrically connected aparatus of proper construction.

Disembodied spirits find in the magnetic somnambulist a perfect means of manifestation. If they desire to communicate by pronunciation, they find in the *somnambule* all necessary qualifications. The lungs are performing their functions by causing natural respiration of air, as well during magnetic slumber as while the subject is in a normal condition. The organs of speech lose none of their necessary development during magnetic influence.

The magnetic power of the spirit desiring to communicate draws from the over-charged organism of the magnetized subject a current of vital electricity, which when concentrated upon the organs of speech, causes them to vibrate in accordance with their (the spirits') intelligence and will power. And in this manner, and through these means, all the varying forms of spirit communications and manifestations are accomplished. The whole phenomena is in accordance with the great universal law of demand and supply. There are many processes of communication, but in all the wide universe there is but one means, and that means is what some term "the medium of sensation," others, "vital energy," "element of sympathy" and vital electricity. I have made use of the latter term, because I believe it best comprehends the idea designed.

CHAPTER XIX.

HOW TO FORM CIRCLES SO AS TO GET COMMUNICATIONS.

WE WILL now proceed to consider how circles should be formed, so as to develop mediums, and avoid misapprehension and discord. I have found that in order to obtain good and noble communications, it is positively necessary that our thoughts and aspirations be also good and elevated. We must be child-like, simple-hearted, manly, open, and free-minded; and these qualifications must be combined with an honest love for truth. Moreover, it is essential that the circles be always organized upon positive and negative principles. Suppose twelve individuals design to form a circle: it is necessary that six of these should be positive and the remaining six negative; and the surest way to arrive at this positive and negative equilibrium is for the twelve to consist of six males and six females. This distinction of male and female is not so essential to be observed, with regard to sex; but six of the number should possess the feminine temperament and attributes of character—which are negative and affectionate—and the others should be decidedly masculine, having the positive and intellectual temperament predominant. Male and female are positive and negative principles; but the terms should not be applied and confined exclusively to mere organization, for some individuals who wear the physical vesture of the male, are, in their characters and temperaments, female, and *vice versa.*

It matters not how few nor how many are connected with a circle, but whatever number there may be, the principle of positive and negative attributes must be regarded in order to receive intelligent communication. Circles formed upon this principle of equilibrium of power will generally result in material manifestations, such as the "raps," table-tipping, and moving of ponderable bodies, and every negative member is unconsciously a medium.

In forming a circle for individual improvement, or development of some individual as a somnambulic medium, it is necessary that certain rules be adhered to. First, the person designing to become a medium must be negative to all the other members of the circle. (A negative temperament is generally indicated by a warm, moist hand, while persons with habitually cold hands are positive.) The medium must be mentally willing to enter the condition sought, in order to attract the magnetic element flowing from the others. They should sit at the head of the table, with their hands resting upon it, the palms downward. The remaining members of the circle must occupy positions corresponding to their temperaments. Those whose positive conditions are indicated by cold hands, should take their position on the right of the medium, and the negative principles on the left. All these like the medium should rest their hands upon the table. Having abided by these rules, it is necessary that those persons who do not desire to be influenced should energetically will that some other individual shall become a medium; and as harmony is imperatively essential to the production of an effect, the individual who is expected to become the medium must be designated, and such designation must be recognized by every member of the circle.

After the medium has been rendered somnambulic by the above means, it is necessary in order to receive communications from disembodied spirits, that perfect harmony should continue to prevail—not only among the members of the circle, but all the assembly as well. There must prevail a unanimity of purpose, in order to avoid a confliction of desires. (I have elsewhere illustrated the probable consequence in such a case.) After it is manifest that the spirits have formed a connection with the medium, the most positive of the circle should make the first demand for communication or manifestation, and this duty should involve upon him in order to avoid the danger of his exerting a counter-influence. Persons who connect themselves with circles should be temperate in all their habits; and it is absolutely necessary that they should be free from all intoxicating or stimulating beverages, for a person who is under the influence of inebriating drinks is a powerful magnet and absorbent of vital magnetism, and such an individual being present in a circle must necessarily greatly retard progress. In fact, I have known the presence of such persons to cause good mediums to be incapable of receiving influence during their stay, and this incapability was in consequence of their absorption of the vital element necessary to cause the magnetic coma of the medium.

The sessions of circles should not be very frequent in occurrence, because those things which become too familiar are thereby deprived of their sanctity, and hence, also, of their power to benefit the assembled individuals. The masses do not always associate respect with familiarity. For this reason it is good for most people that "angels' visits are few and far between," becau e were they of frequent occurrence, and as common as sunlight, many minds, I regret to say, would not only fall into a state of ingratitude, but they would neglect to properly appreciate the perpetual blessings flowing therefrom. Therefore, it is necessary to avoid a too great intimacy.

These sessions should be conducted with perfect dignity and harmony; but these conditions should not be allowed to prohibit a genial flow of appropriate conversation, or cheerful, intelligent mirth. Harmonial music is a great benefit to a circle, inasmuch as it banishes discord. These assemblages, to be successful, must be indeed, and in sentiment, harmonial circles, entirely devoid of jarring discord. Carry not into them any unkind feelings, nor sensations of envy or jealousy. Let no feelings of unforgiveness against a fellow being mar the spotless beauty of your soul. But, above all, remember that the mind, the soul, the spirit, has no particular Sunday habiliment—that you cannot adorn it with a clean, shining vesture as you may the body—but as you clothe it for every-day life, so will it go adorned to the sanctuary of spirit intercourse.

The rooms where the circles meet should, as much as possible, be retired from all discordant noise and interruption ; and it is also a great benefit to have the rooms darkened, so that the persons present, not having their minds attracted and diverted by external things, may the more easily concentrate their thoughts upon the object for which they have met together.

The above is the usual mode of developing mediums; but beside these means there are others which may be employed with good effect. For instance, a simple magnetic cord has been found to be a most powerful assistant to medial development. There are many kinds of these in use, but the simplest, cheapest, and to my mind the best, is made and used in the following manner: Get a piece of half inch rope some five yards in length and cover it with cotton velvet; take this rope thus prepared, and wind around it, parallel with each other, two wires, one of zinc or steel, and the other of silver or copper; these wires should be wound so as to be about a quarter of an inch apart. The circle should sit uniformly around the table, and let the magnetic cord lie on their laps, their hands upon or grasping it. The person who is the most positive should grasp one end of the cord firmly in his left hand, and the one who is designed to become the medium should sit on his left and next to him, with the other end of the cord grasped in his right hand. Another way is to only rest one hand upon the cord, while the other rests upon the table. If these rules are complied with, it will not be long before the person designed to be influenced—if he or she are constitutionally susceptible to magnetic influx—will feel a throbbing in the hands, and ultimately, by repeated trials, they will in all probability be rendered somnambulic, and if their organism is sufficiently refined, and their mental powers appropriately balanced, they may even become clairvoyants.

Proper manipulations will greatly augment the mesmeric tendency of an impressible subject. In fact, I have known persons to be developed as spiritual mediums by these manipulating processes alone.

The *modus operandi* of developing mediums is so well known at the present time that it is hardly necessary to refer to the subject at all. The reason why mediums are not more readily developed is owing much to the erroneous idea that disembodied spirits have the power of producing magnetic influence. Let impressible individuals remember that the means of spirit communication all emanate from terrestrial sources—from surrounding organisms, and let them act in accordance with these facts, and they will find that the desired end will be more easily accomplished. Many suppose that all are capable of becoming mediums, but I consider this supposition in part to be incorrect. I estimate that, by the employment of ordinary means, one in fifty can become mediums; and that one in five hundred of these, who may be mediums, can, by persistent endeavors become somnambulists; and of these one in a thousand may be clairvoyants or seers.

This estimate as regards somnambulic mediums, may be too low, or at least, may be so considered by the careless observer. There are many who claim to be somnambulic mediums, who in reality are not. The communications received through such mediums (meaning those who really are not somnambulists,) will invariably betray a local origin, and their expressions of intelligence generally correspond to their preconceived ideas. Such mediums need development, and the only way to develop them is to increase the magnetic influence sufficiently to render them mentally unconscious.

It has not been my design to prove that spirits do communicate (for of the facts of such occurrences thousands are already convinced by unimpeachable evidence), but to furnish a philosophical explanation of the manner in which they do communicate. Hence I have sought no individual's testimonies, because the manifestations now before the world constitute one grand living demonstration that spirits do communicate with mankind.

There are two distinct kinds of communication received from spirits. First, such as emanate from spirits who have in the circle relatives, according to the law of natural consanguinity. These are generally messages of affectionate remembrance and regard, they are characteristically like the friendly intercourse between relatives in the body; hence, to the fortuitous and inappreciative observer they ofttimes appear child-like and insipid. But they are none the less genuine manifestations of spirit intelligence, for being displays of intellectual medriocity. Spirits vary in knowledge as well as men. If they are infinite then they are equal to God; but if they are not infinite, then they are subject to the law of gradation the same as man; and if they are subject to the law of gradation, why should we wonder at their display of intellectual frivolty any more than we do the intellectual and moral frivolties of man. Perhaps you may say that spirits have something better to employ themselves with—some occupation above these apparently vapid manifestations. I do not doubt but what they have. So has the man of extended knowledge a nobler field of operation, yet we often find him engaged in an almost vapid display of intellectual frivolty. Dignity is no sign of intellectuality. The truly intellectual ofttimes betray the greatest simplicity of manner. Spirits are beings of affection, who are subject to the law of sympathy the same as man in the body. Sympathy is the main spring of social intercourse, and without it, heaven would be a hell.

The second class of spirits who communicate with mankind are those who design the aggrandizement of the whole human family. Their missions are to wage war against the superstitions of ignorance, the fanaticisms of creed-bound mortals, and the bigotry of sanctimonious, self-righteous subjects of eternal progress. To come in communicative rapport with these spirits of intelligence, the circles formed should press forward to the attainments of knowledge; no fetters of creed and doctrine should stay their steps in progression. Truth will lead them into the broad fields of infinitude—into the illimitable expanse of nature. If we would advance in knowledge we must not weary in our investigations, nor let the hot shots of bigotry and superstition arrest the minds for searching after God. We must not clasp close the clasps of our Bibles, and say thus far will I go, and no farther, in my search after truth. Nor must we rest contented with mere words; for they are but the drapery of truths, the shrouds which "darkeneth counsel." Words cannot set bounds to thought, nor can creeds satisfy the longings of a progressive mind. The undying soul shall be taught forever from the everlasting volumes of Nature, as one after another they unfold to its growing capacity. Nature is the ever open pages of God's eternal word; it is a book which is never closed, never "clasped with a clasp," and from this book spirits would teach us the ways of life, and the certainty of immortal existence.

Many imagine that spiritualism is opposed to the true religion of Christ; but such is not the case. It only opposes the bigotry of the Church, the fanaticism and illiberality of creeds. It endeavors to tear away the mask of superstition, which for past ages has enveloped like a shroud, the beauty and simplicity of the Christian religion. It wages war against the blasphemous and absurd doctrine of moral degradation. It teaches us that man is by nature pure—by education vile. It teahces us to properly appreciate every endowment of our nature, both spiritual and physical. We are taught by spirits the reasonable doctrine of eternal progression; and that a perfect physical organization is necessary to spirit advancement here in rudimental life, and that if we would grow in grace, we must obey all the laws of our being. In short, it teaches us that this earth—this primary existence—is the spirit's first sphere of action—the beginning of eternity, and if we are in harmony with the laws of our exisience, it is the all-sufficient though progressive heaven prepared by the Almighty Giver of good gifts alone. Spirits teach us that physical death is the beginning of a purer spiritual life.

These are a few of the great lessons the angels come to teach us. Let those who have hitherto looked upon death as a dark abyss—as the termination of personal identification, come and behold the beautiful light that now illumines those once supposed impenetrable depths. Spirits by their teachings have literally robbed the grave of its gloom. So those who love life need grieve no more, when the years of life fly past them; let them no more be saddened when they are gone; let them not cling to those years as the drowning mariner grasps at a board, because they are life to us, and that life is to be cherished. To the spiritualist, the darkness of death is made luminous; light, radiant light, to-day penetrates the unfathomable darkness of religion and mythology; the black pall of ignorance is being lifted from mortal vision—the bright sun of heaven drives away the thick mists of past ages, and now the soul can look far, far into eternity, and behold that to the spirit there is no death. By the increasing light of spiritualism the human mind penetrates deeper, and deeper into the forever extending future—into the innumerable abysses of the universe, and sees everywhere the glowing gems of truth; nor do the boundless riches which it contemplates cause it to reject one, even the least, of those which it once gathered from the years of past experience. Nay, for they too were jewels, given by the hand of the Almighty, and are therefore imperishable. Nothing of all God's treasury can be lost; hence we need not fear that a single truth will ever be cast away, or that aught that is in the future can be destroyed. Aye, the beautiful truths of spiritualism reveal to us the glorious fact that from everlasting, to everlasting, we are the children of God, and ever objects of Divine love.

It is often remarked that this modern phenomena of spiritualism is only a novel phase of the art of magnetism. This remark is literally correct. The art of magnetism furnishes the means of spirit communication; for it is the main spring of spirit manifestation.

Therefore, to properly appreciate this truly natural phenomena, it is necessary for us to make deep research into the mysteries of nature's universal medium of sensation and agent of sympathetic connection—"magnetism." A perfect knowledge of the attributes of this element of vital power will furnish a magic key to unlock nature's store-house of mystery. The Almighty manifests His will by means of this agent, and we have seen that it was *this* that gave the spirit of man control of physical nature; by this agent the spirit manifests its existence, both in the body and out. Thus we make spiritualism a science.

INDEX.

CHAPTER I.

CHAPTER II.

CHAPTER III.

CHAPTER IV.

CHAPTER V.

CHAPTER VI.

CHAPTER VII.

CHAPTER VIII.

CHAPTER IX.

CHAPTER X.

CHAPTER XI.

CHAPTER XII.

CHAPTER XIII.

CHAPTER XIV.

CHAPTER XV.

CHAPTER XVI.

CHAPTER XVII.

CHAPTER XVIII.

CHAPTER XIX.

www.ingramcontent.com/pod-product-compliance
Lightning Source LLC
LaVergne TN
LVHW011217110826
845150LV00006B/1448

* 9 7 8 1 4 2 5 5 1 7 2 9 8 *